To the Morgan's all ...).

HAUNTED
LONG ISLAND
MYSTERIES

Kerriann Flanagan Brosky
4/7/22

KERRIANN FLANAGAN BROSKY

FOREWORD BY JOE GIAQUINTO

HAUNTED
AMERICA

Published by Haunted America
A division of The History Press
Charleston, SC
www.historypress.com

All images are author's collection, unless otherwise noted.

First published 2021

Manufactured in the United States

ISBN 9781467144346

Library of Congress Control Number: 2021941092

To those I loved and lost in 2020.

Author and friend Dr. Alfred V. Sforza
April 1, 2020

Author and best friend from childhood Karen R. Steinberg
May 10, 2020

One of my biggest fans, my uncle, Sean P. Flanagan
May 12, 2020

My beloved mother, Deanna M. Flanagan, my best friend
and the strongest person I will ever know
December 30, 2020

Books by Kerriann Flanagan Brosky

Huntington's Hidden Past

Huntington's Past Revisited

Ghosts of Long Island: Stories of the Paranormal

Ghosts of Long Island II: More Stories of the Paranormal

Delectable Italian Dishes for Family and Friends,
co-authored with Sal Baldanza

The Medal, a novel

Historic Haunts of Long Island:
Ghost and Legends from the Gold Coast to Montauk Point

Historic Crimes of Long Island: Misdeeds from the 1600s to the 1950s

IN ADDITION

The Ghostly Tales of Long Island by Rachel Kempster Barry,
adapted from *Historic Haunts of Long Island* for Middle Grade Readers

CONTENTS

FOREWORD

Nothing in life is to be feared, it is only to be understood.
Now is the time to understand more, so that we may fear less.
—Marie Curie

During my work with Kerriann on her book projects, our journey evolved—it became more spiritual. In *Haunted Long Island Mysteries*, Kerriann's latest compendium of historic, ghostly places, this evolution continues with new investigation methods and ghost-hunting tools.

For example, several stories now include my impressions as a psychic-medium. Psychic ability reads the energy of a person or place, to gain knowledge of things, while mediumship is the ability to talk with those in spirit through our intuitive senses of seeing, hearing and feeling. Incorporating these skills in our investigations has helped us corroborate stories of paranormal activity from eyewitnesses.

In our field work, we've always used a few simple, high-tech devices, including cameras, a ghost meter and digital audio recorders. While we still rely heavily on our cameras to find orbs and apparitions, and the ghost meter to locate hauntings, we've changed our audio recording device of choice to the ghost box—a special type of radio.

Spirits use two methods to generate vocal responses from the ghost box. One is by using white noise from the static found between radio stations along the frequency band. The second is human voice, spoken during on-air broadcasts from talk shows, advertisements, weather reports, sporting events and newscasts. Human voice provides the foundation for clear, high-quality answers from the other side. And most importantly—the conversations are live, in real time.

In the future, can we expect technology to talk to the spirit world on demand, using a combination of holographic and synthesized speech gadgetry? The use of the ghost-box radio in Kerriann's new book might offer us a glimmer of this future reality.

One of the coolest features in all of her ghost books is the ability to read a chapter and then go online and listen to the spirit recordings for yourself. These noncorporeal communicators can be quite entertaining, as they comment on various subjects and answer questions we pose to them.

In addition to the spirit recordings, you'll find several excellent photos showing paranormal occurrences such as orbs and apparitions throughout the text.

There is truly magic to the exploration of the supernatural world! From jaunts into graveyards and old mansions to intelligent communication with people from the past, each chapter is an exciting journey of discovery—with some mystery and surprises thrown in. And every story is backed by credible historical research, live interviews and analysis of the evidence we gathered during each expedition.

There is something for everyone in this book. If you love history, it's in the book. If you like to read ghost stories and urban legends, there are many to peruse here. And if you've ever been curious how a paranormal researcher does their work, you'll find it here as well.

—Joe Giaquinto
medium and paranormal investigator

PREFACE

But if I have succeeded in opening only one closed mind just a fraction to the very real possibility that objective "ghosts" do indeed exist, or if only one sceptic decides to seek for him [or her] self to become a ghost hunter, then my journey into these difficult regions will not have been in vain.
—*Peter Underwood,* Ghosts and How to See Them

My fascination with ghosts began at an early age. As I pursued trying to understand them, I was inspired by author and parapsychologist Peter Underwood from England and Austrian American author and parapsychologist Hanz Holzer. My own work has been greatly influenced by Peter Underwood, specifically his ten types of ghosts. Ghosts cannot be defined as any one thing. It is more complex than that. Hollywood's versions of ghosts are usually frightening, demonic specters out to possess the next victim. I have spent the last fifteen years of my life undoing this very unrealistic belief.

For those of you familiar with my work, you may know that this is my fourth "ghost" book out of the nine books I have written. The journey of investigating over one hundred presumably haunted locales on Long Island, has led me to understand many things, including the importance of these spiritual beings and how they relate to our past and history, to the continuity of life after death and to the ability to communicate with our loved ones after they have passed. It is a far cry to what is often viewed on TV and in the theater.

My books have evolved over the years, and while weaving in important historical information about treasured places on Long Island, my books have become more spiritual.

In reading *Haunted Long Island Mysteries*, you will learn a great deal about our Revolutionary War past, maritime history, political figures, artists and socialites.

On the chapter about genre artist William Sidney Mount, who died in 1868, you will read the continuing story of the fascinating relationship Joe Giaquinto and I have developed with Mr. Mount throughout the years.

You will also read about real people from today who have made contact with those who have crossed to the other side. The last story in the book is about Rebecca, a remarkable young equestrian who died tragically in 2016. Originally part of a story I was writing on Sundance Stables, Rebecca's story is so profound that I wrote it as a separate chapter that reveals the amazing connections she has had with her parents since her death.

Joe and I are not trying to prove or disprove anything that appears in this book. We are simply putting our research and investigations out there for one to ponder, while at the same time, teaching you about local history and the importance of preserving it.

In closing, much of this book was written during the extraordinary times of the coronavirus pandemic. Many of you may be suffering immense losses and grief. I hope if nothing else, my book will bring you some comfort in knowing our loved ones are not that far away. They are safe and happy and watching over us. All you need to do is be open.

—Kerriann Flanagan Brosky

AUTHOR'S NOTE

This book is made to give readers an interactive experience. Many of the chapters contain segments of ghost box recording sessions. If you would like to listen to the actual recordings for yourself while reading the short transcripts visit www.ghostsoflongisland.com and click on *Haunted Long Island Mysteries*.

ACKNOWLEDGEMENTS

Abig thank-you goes out to all of the people I have interviewed who
have shared their remarkable stories with me and also to all those
who assisted me with historical research. I am most grateful.

Ann W. Latner, education director, Cow Neck Peninsula Historical Society;
Amy Dzija Driscoll, director, North Shore Historical Museum; Barbara
M. Russell, town historian for the Town of Brookhaven; Bob and Anna
McCarroll; Butch Yamali, president and CEO, Dover Restaurant Group;
Craig and Ryan Sweezey; Denice Sheppard, director, Oyster Bay Historical
Society; Diane Schwindt, director, Smith Estate at Longwood; Doris
DeQuinzio, Locust Valley Library; Frank Giebfried, trustee, Bayport–Blue
Point Historical Association; Fred and Pat Blumlein, Cow Neck Peninsula
Historical Society; Gloria Rocchio, president, Ward Melville Heritage
Organization; Hans Henke, Patchogue Village historian; Jeanie and Gerard
Leonard; Karen Petz; Kathy Jones, Locust Valley Library; Kathy Smith,
director, Locust Valley Library; Kim Voyages; Kym Turet; Lauren Wallach,
Locust Valley Library; Leanne Berg, vice president, Bayport-Blue Point
Historical Association; Lynne and Eric Weissbard, Sundance Stables; Mary
Cascone, Town of Babylon historian; Maria and Tom Carson, owners,
Farm Country Kitchen; Michael Colucci, property manager, Ward Melville
Heritage Association; Milleridge Inn employees Sara Anne Huenke, Terry
Wilson, Elena Saitta, Karen Ascencio; Nadia Russo; Richard Martin,
director of historic services, Suffolk County Parks; Robyn Silvestri; Terry
Lister-Blitman, executive director, Long Island Maritime Museum; Thomas

Rizzuto, Locust Valley Library; Tony Garro; Wendy Polhemus-Annibell, head research librarian, Suffolk County Historical Society Library Archives.

To my acquisition editor, J. Banks Smither, for his willingness to take on another ghost book project and for his continued support of my work as an author.

To my team of editors, public relations liaisons and sales and marketing specialists at The History Press/Arcadia Publishing for all of the hard work they do behind the scenes.

To my sons, Ryan and Patrick, for giving me the space I need to continue my work.

To my husband, Karl, who has survived nine book deadlines with me. Thank you for your love and unfailing support, for being the first read for all my books and for helping me with all things technical. Most of all, thanks for always believing in me.

To Joe Giaquinto, aka "Mulder," for all you have taught me about ghost investigating and spiritual communication. I will always treasure our adventures from the sixteen years we have been working together and all that we have discovered and learned.

1

MILLERIDGE INN

JERICHO

The Milleridge Inn in Jericho does not hide the fact that the iconic Long Island restaurant, which is one of the oldest continually operating food establishments in the United States, is indeed haunted. In fact, it has even created a slogan: "We have everything for you at the Milleridge Inn, including ghosts."

Having investigated several haunted restaurants over the years, I have to say that ghosts are good for business. The Milleridge has even taken it a step further, and has created a "haunted village" that people can walk through every Halloween. The Milleridge Inn has been extremely "active" for many years, and unexplained phenomena abound.

The inn was originally built in 1672 as a private home. The two-room, clapboard, shingled house was built on a rugged fieldstone foundation and had a large central fireplace, which still exists today. It was built for Mary Washburn Willets, who was the widowed sister-in-law of Robert Williams, who founded Jericho. The Willets were Quakers who farmed the lands around Jericho and who led very quiet and religious lives. When the American Revolution began, the Hessian and British officers took occupancy of Mary's home, where they remained for approximately eight years. After the war, Jericho began to flourish, and it became an important stopover for travelers passing through. By 1815, Jericho Turnpike was formed, and the old Willets home was used as an inn. Travelers dined on home-baked bread, meat, fish and stews. By 1890, the inn was expanded and then was sold to the Doughty family, who owned nearby Jericho Cider Mill. At one point, the home served as a boardinghouse for Jericho schoolteachers.

By 1937, Percy L. Roberts decided to lease the building and turned it into a restaurant called the Maine Maid Inn and Tea Room. Roberts decided to buy the building in 1950, but the operators of the Maine Maid Inn refused to sell. A few years later, the business moved across the road to the old Valentine Hicks home, where it remained as a restaurant until 2007.

The Miller family started a new business at the original location and called their new restaurant Mille Ridge. By 1961, James Murphy purchased the building and ten acres and changed the name of the restaurant to the Milleridge Inn. It was at this time that the colonial village, so loved by Long Islanders today, was created.

For over fifty years, the Milleridge Inn was owned and operated by the Murphy family, with Owen Smith, the son-in-law of the Murphys', at the helm. At the end of 2015, Owen, at seventy-eight years old, was set to retire. The fate of the Milleridge Inn was unknown. There were rumors that the iconic restaurant would be torn down. The business was sold to Kimco Realty, which was a New Hyde Park–based real estate investment company that owned several strip malls. Concerned citizens started a petition and a "Save the Milleridge" Facebook page. Meanwhile, Owen Smith, in a desperate search, worked with Kimco representatives to try to find someone who would keep the beloved building and grounds as a restaurant and village. Butch Yamali, president and CEO of the Dover restaurant group, stepped forward and decided to purchase the Milleridge Inn. Not only was the building saved, but also seventy-five employees got to keep their jobs. Butch Yamail's vision was to restore the Milleridge Inn to its original luster.

The Milleridge Inn is a stately white clapboard structure in which a number of architectural styles can be seen, including the classic colonial style in the oldest section of the house, as well as the Victorian style, which is evident in the parlor wing. An interesting feature is the tap room, which was originally a windbreak for the main house and was used as both a barn and a buttery. The old windbreak was used as the frame of the current day tap room.

Along with its architectural charm, the décor and flavor of the original homestead has remained and includes such details as wide plank flooring, low ceilings and exposed beams. There are many floors and rooms at Milleridge, and they are decorated and furnished in authentic eighteenth- and nineteenth-century styles.

Milleridge Inn.

The menu reflects the past as well, and classic American cuisine is served. Yankee pot roast, roast turkey with sage stuffing, prime rib and stuffed filet of sole are some of the more traditional, popular items, and delicious fresh baked bread and popovers are made on the premises. The colonial village boasts the Bread and Jam Shop, the General Store and Murphy's Florist, among other shops, and elsewhere on the premises is a cottage and carriage house that is used for catering.

It was a dreary, rainy Monday when Joe and I set out to interview several of the employees about their experiences and conduct our own investigation. Joe arrived first and was greeted by Sara Anne Huenke, director of marketing and promotions, who took him around the tiny village. As they walked around, Joe saw a figure of a man leaning into the window of the General Store. The village was closed that day, and no one was working in the store. Joe had a very strong sense that the British had once roamed the property. He did not know anything prior about the British soldiers occupying the house.

Sara and Joe made their way up to the inn where I was waiting. It was morning, so only a few employees were there. We went up a flight of stairs to the Quaker Room, where we would conduct the first of many interviews that day.

Sara Anne started working for the Dover Group and the Milleridge in August 2018. Many of the employees had told her they've had experiences at the inn, generally late at night or very early in the morning when all the customers are gone. Although Sara Anne had only been working at the Milleridge for a few months, she admitted that she constantly gets orbs in all of the photos she takes there, especially in the cottage when they are having events. She told us that many guests capture orbs in the restaurant as well.

"We had an Elvis night recently, and whoever was here liked Elvis because they [the orbs] were everywhere," Sara Anne explained.

Later, when I was transcribing the interview with Sara Anne, I captured an EVP. As soon as Sara Anne had said the orbs were everywhere, I heard a voice say, "Oh, wow." There was only Joe, Sara Anne and me in the room at the time of the interview.

General manager Terry Wilson joined us a few minutes later and told us about the first night he worked at Milleridge: "When I first started here in September 2018, my first night here by myself, I heard about the [ghost] stories, and I was completely freaked out because I had to lock the building by myself that first night. I literally said to myself, 'I can't do this.' Since then, though, I have taken the whole ghost thing lightly."

Terry told me about an article he had stumbled upon from a blog that was posted in October 2011. The blogger's sister had apparently worked at the Milleridge Inn during the 1980s. Terry had been told that sometime during the years when it was a private home, there was a fire, and several family members were killed. According to the article, the top floor bedrooms were destroyed and had to be rebuilt. No year was given, but it was assumed to be in the late 1800s. I did research, but I came up with nothing that could support this story. The only mention of a fire at the Milleridge was a kitchen fire in 2014. The story of the fire and the family perishing was possibly passed along throughout the years, but it cannot be documented as truth.

The blogger said that his sister did not like going into a very tiny room on the second floor that at one time might have been used as a nursery since there was a small crib and a chair there. She claimed that the room was always ice cold and that other employees felt uncomfortable in the room as well. This room today is known as the bridal suite. A manager who worked there at that time claimed he would hear footsteps approaching his office on the second floor, but when he went to the door, no one was there. He also had the feeling of being watched. A painting crew also had feelings of being watched on the second floor and felt a cold breeze pass by numerous times. As the story goes, one of the painters was left alone upstairs late at night while the other painter went downstairs to get a cup of coffee. While he was alone, he had the sensation of being stared at. He turned to look and saw a man, woman and a little boy standing at the end of the hallway staring at him.

Although the story cannot be proven, thirty years later, employees are still experiencing unexplained things on the second floor, including in the small room and in the office.

Some of the Spanish-speaking employees had told Sara Anne about "la niña," which means "the girl" in Spanish. Apparently, the ghost of a little girl has made her presence known on the main floor. People can feel her energy, and several others have heard her laughing or have heard footsteps like those of a child's.

The little girl isn't the only one haunting the inn. One employee we spoke with always sees a woman sitting in the bay window of the main restaurant looking out, while others claim to have seen a male figure there. Another employee, Kristin, told us of an incident that happened just two weeks before our arrival.

"One of the girls from the office was bringing a lady up to show her one of the rooms," said Kristin. "And when the employee went up the stairs, she

Main dining room with bay window where a ghostly woman and male figure have been seen.

said she saw a ghost, a woman all in black at the top of the stairs. She said there was no face. She saw just the silhouette."

Strange things have even occurred in the restrooms. Toilets have been known to start flushing on their own in the upstairs bathrooms when no one is there. Those particular toilets do not have any sensors to set them off.

There is another story about a male manager and a female server who were closing up one night. Everyone was gone and most of the lights were out. The server went into the restroom on the first floor before heading home. The manager turned and saw a man walk in after her, so he ran in, and nobody was there but the server.

One of the spookiest stories told to us that day was from Elena Saitta, the banquet manager:

> *Over the summer the restaurant was closed every Monday. We would still be here working until 6:00 p.m. Most of the employees' offices were in the village, but my office was in here. Everyone would say to me, "You're going to work in there by yourself?" It was the daytime, and I told them I'd be fine. So, I was staying a little later and it's around 6:10 p.m., and I have the front door locked and the back door locked. I was the only person in this building. Nobody else was here. I heard a door open, and I assumed it was Pam because she had a set of keys. So, I keep working, but she did not walk into my office. So I called out to her, and she didn't answer. Then I looked at her appointment book and saw that she had an appointment at the cottage at that time. I tried calling her, but she always forgets to take her cell phone. So, I keep trying, and all of a sudden, doors start slamming. A bunch of them. I was just sitting there. I couldn't even move I was so scared.*
>
> *I then sent her a text message and said, "Pam, you to need to come and remove me from the building. I'm so scared I can't even stand up." The doors stopped slamming for a few minutes, but then it started up again. And I mean slamming. Loud noises. I couldn't move. In our office there is a window—it's like a sheer curtain that looks out into the dining room. So, I'm staring out of it when I see a dark image literally sprinting back and forth in the dining room. I was so scared that I didn't want to leave. I didn't want to walk through there. Pam wasn't answering, and I started crying. I said to myself, I just have to do it. I have to get out of here. I left my desk, took one step out of the office and then I started running all the way from my office to the front door, to the village and to Pam's office. All the things that have happened here are usually at times when people are not in the building.*

While Joe and I were interviewing Elena in the Garden Room, the wall sconce behind her kept flickering. We decided to get the ghost box up and running, and we made connection almost immediately. Here is a portion of our transcript:

> *Joe: Elena, you want to say hello to them?*
> *Elena: Hello, spirits.*
> *Spirit: Elena.*
> *Joe: I think I heard, "Elena."*
> *Spirit: Great!*
> *Kerriann: We had gotten energy. Is it from the little girl in the Garden Room?*
> *Spirit: Who's that?*
> *Spirit: Who are you?*
> *Spirit: This time, she's dead.*
> *Spirit: Me!*
> *Joe: Me. I heard me.*
> *Kerriann: Is the little girl that got burned in the fire with us today?*
> *Spirit: Hi.*
> *Joe: I think she said, "Hi."*
> *Spirit: Love you!*
> *Kerriann: Are you here with us?*
> *Spirit: Yes.*
> *Spirit: Of course.* [British accent heard.]

Next up we interviewed Karen Ascencio, who had been a banquet manager at Milleridge for sixteen years.

"I never believed in anything until I started working at the Milleridge Inn," Karen said. "I had been working as a cashier when I first started here, and it was the first time I had to close out. I went upstairs to drop off the money in the office, and I came back down the little ramp and went into the bathroom. A minute later, I heard the door open and heard the sound of somebody blowing their nose. When I came out of the stall and went over to wash my hands, all of a sudden—" Karen paused. "I'm getting the chills right now just thinking about it."

She continued,

> *While I was in the bathroom, I suddenly felt an icy cold. I stood there and turned around and I said, "Hello? Hello?" I'm looking under the*

stalls to see if anybody was there and there wasn't. I came running downstairs, and I was freaking out. I was so scared. The manager that was closing said, "What happened?" Then he asked me if I saw her. I said to him, "What are you talking about? Did I see who?" He said, "The little girl. Did you see her?" I just started crying. He told me that he had actually seen her in the Quaker Room. Since then, I've seen her in the Philodendron Room. She wears a little white dress. Another time while I was in the Willets Room early in the morning I heard laughing, and it was just me and the manager. She [the little girl] *doesn't like change. If anything is changed, things happen.*

Besides the ghosts that roam the old inn, there are spirits who pop in just to say hello. One of them, we believe, was a man by the name of William "Billy" Cahoon, a longtime customer and friend of the employees at the Milleridge Inn. According to Terry Wilson, Billy had dinner at the Milleridge every Friday and Saturday night for twenty-eight years. He was a seventy-year-old retired school janitor who lived alone and was adored by those who worked at the restaurant. In December 2018, Billy did not show up for dinner, and the employees became concerned.

"He was a very simple man," recalled Terry. "We started getting concerned when he didn't come in the following week. He didn't have a credit card. He paid in cash. We didn't even know his last name. By the third week, Brendan, the manager, said we had to find out what was going on with him. So, we contacted the taxi company that he always took, and through that, we were able to get his address in Levittown. Brendan went over there early one morning and knocked on the door. No one answered. He found a side door unlocked, and as soon as he opened it, by the smell, he knew that he had died. He called the police."

On January 4, 2019, homicide detectives had determined that William Cahoon had been stabbed more than ten times and had been dead for a month.

In June 2019, David Cahoon of Melville, the forty-year-old nephew of Billy Cahoon, was arrested and charged with second-degree murder. Apparently, David Cahoon was down on his luck and in need of money. He came to his uncle, and when Billy did not give it to him, he killed him.

At the time of our investigation, which was on March 25, 2019, the murderer was not yet known. We had headed over to the bridal suite, which as mentioned earlier, is a sensitive area of the house, and the ghost meter I had been holding started beeping. Joe had recorded this on video. After the

Painting of the little girl believed to haunt the Milleridge Inn.

beeping stopped, Joe played back the video, and an orb was seen flying past me. It was in this room that Terry had told us the story about Billy Cahoon. With the ghost box running, we made a brief connection with Mr. Cahoon. When Joe said, "Mr. Cahoon?" the spirit repeated back, "Cahoon." Terry then asked Billy if it was him and if he was around. The spirit replied, "I am grateful for the laughter." It seemed to us that Billy Cahoon was at peace and that he was grateful for the years he had spent dining at the restaurant.

The employees of the Milleridge Inn have come to terms with the unexplained activity that goes on there, and like many people in these situations, they have learned to coexist with the ghosts. The Milleridge Inn remains a happy and heartwarming restaurant that is loved by all who enter it. Thanks to a dedicated team, the Milleridge Inn, and its resident ghosts, are here to stay.

2

BREWSTER HOUSE

SETAUKET

The Brewster House in Setauket, also known as the Joseph Brewster House, was built circa 1665 and is the oldest house in the town of Brookhaven. This saltbox-style home was originally a one-room cottage that had been expanded five times throughout the seventeenth, eighteenth and nineteenth centuries. It is located on Route 25A, a busy thoroughfare that was once a Native American trail. When the settlers came in 1665, they turned the trail into a road and called it Kings Highway. It is now referred to as Washington's Spy Trail.

Reverend Nathaniel Brewster came to Setauket from England not long after the British settlement of Setauket. He became the town's first ordained minister and served the Presbyterian congregation until his death in 1690. The house in which he lived consisted of one small room with a fireplace, which was used as a living room, dining room and kitchen. A garret upstairs was used for sleeping space. The large fireplace is where meals were cooked, and it also provided the only source of heat for the home.

Records show that Nathaniel had three sons, but only Timothy and Daniel came across with him to America. His oldest son, John, had remained in England. It was Timothy who inherited the house and approximately ten acres after his father's death, and he expanded it so that it could accommodate his wife, Mary Hawkins, and their seven children. The expansion took place in the early 1700s, when an almost identical house was placed next to the original seventeenth-century room. The center chimney and framing elements were rebuilt so that the houses could be joined together, creating a home nearly doubled in size. Daniel lived nearby and had inherited a second home lot, which his father had purchased from John Roe. Both Timothy and Daniel became prominent figures in the Brookhaven Town government, each having served as town clerk at various times.

The youngest of Timothy's children, Joseph Brewster, inherited the family homestead after Timothy's death, circa 1741. Joseph served as town justice and was also one of Setauket's early innkeepers. Records indicate that Joseph was granted a license to keep "A Publick House of Entertaiment" and to "sell strong drink or liquors by retaile in the house where he now dwelleth." Turning one's home into an inn was not uncommon in its day. Since early settlements were few and far between, licenses were granted to turn homes into taverns, general stores and inns where homeowners could provide food and lodging to travelers.

Joseph and his wife, Ruth Briscoe, had five children there—four girls and a boy. It was during this time that the house was enlarged by a lean-to addition, with a low, sweeping roofline, giving it the saltbox farmhouse look popular of colonial New England. The lean-to addition more than likely served as a pantry. By this time, the house comprised five smaller rooms attached to the back façade. Joseph, who also served the town as a tailor, lived in the house and ran it as an inn until his death in 1760.

Brewster House.

Joseph's son, known as Joseph the Younger, was next in line after his father's death. Joseph, like many of his descendants, was a prominent figure, having served as a lieutenant in the French and Indian War, and later a justice and trustee of the town of Brookhaven. He, like his father, operated a tavern out of the house. He reluctantly entertained British soldiers during the Revolutionary War in order to save his farm from being destroyed or confiscated by the British. He did not trust the British and had installed a barricade at the door at night to prevent surprise visits from them.

Along with the tavern, he ran a general store next to the house. Joseph the Younger was known to give generously to the Patriot cause and was the first cousin of Caleb Brewster, of Culper Spy Ring fame. Caleb, a whaleboat captain, was a junior officer of the Setauket Spies, which was composed of a group of Patriots organized by Major Benjamin Tallmadge, who served under General George Washington. Setauket Harbor, a cove located behind the Brewster House, was one of six locations where Caleb would bring his whaleboat. He would obtain secret information from Manhattan and then cross the Long Island Sound from Setauket to Black Rock, Connecticut, near Bridgeport, where he would deliver the important messages, including the movements of the British troops. Along with delivering the secret information, Caleb is said to have been an expert on guerilla warfare. He would lead men on raids across the island, where they would pillage and attack British ships at night.

As for Joseph, after the Revolutionary War was over, he was given 750 acres by the newly formed American government, and he built a sizable estate. As a thank you, he loaned 300 pounds to the Continental Congress in 1781.

During his time in the house, Joseph married three times and had nine children, all from his first wife, Rebecca Mills. After Joseph the Younger's death in 1818, his two youngest sons, John and William Mills Brewster, inherited the family homestead, and son Samuel inherited the north end of the dwelling house for ten years. John, for reasons unknown, relinquished his claim for his portion.

At the time of Joseph's death, there were three generations of Brewsters living in the house: his third wife, Lucretia Overton; son William Mills and his wife, Juliana, and their two children (Joseph's grandchildren); and son Samuel. It is believed that further expansion of the house in the Federal period may have taken place during the time of their occupancy.

William Mills Brewster and Juliana Dickerson were married in 1804, and they had a son, also named William Mills, and a daughter named Martha.

The son, William Mills, died at age seventeen in 1832. William Mills Brewster Sr. died in 1854 at age seventy-four and had bequeathed half of his real estate to daughter Martha Brewster Willsie and the other half to his granddaughter, Mary. It was stated in the will that his wife, Juliana, should be allowed to stay in the house for the remainder of her life. Juliana died at age eighty-two in 1863.

Daughter Martha had been widowed by her husband, Captain Benjamin T. Willsie, sometime before 1850. While he was alive, Captain Willsie kept the Brewster tradition of innkeeper alive by becoming the first proprietor of the Port Jefferson Hotel.

Martha's daughter, Mary Willsie, married John R. Davis in 1860 at the age of twenty-three. They had five children and continued to live in the family home. Mary Willsie Davis died in 1877, and John died in 1922. On the death of their father, two of the unmarried children, Isaac M. Davis and Mary H. Davis, inherited the home and approximately ten acres. Sometime before 1941, the brother and sister sold six acres. Isaac died in 1936, and Mary H. died in 1947. Mary's will from 1941 stated that upon her death the estate would be inherited by her sister, Cornelia. Cornelia died before Mary, but the will had not been changed. The estate was then passed down to Mary's niece and nephew, Jennie E. Smith and Robert B. Elderkin, the children of Cornelia.

A year later, Jennie and Robert sold the house and four acres to Ward Melville, who owned the house and property until 1970. Melville then deeded it to the Stony Brook Community Fund, which is now called the Ward Melville Heritage Organization.

Seven generations of Brewsters and three generations of Davises had lived in the house. When Mary H. Davis died in 1947, the house still did not have plumbing, electricity, central heat or any other modern amenities.

With a history as rich as this one, Joe and I were excited to visit and conduct our investigation to see if we could connect with those who had lived there. As far as we knew, no one had claimed to have had any paranormal-type experiences in the house prior.

Gloria Rocchio, president of the Ward Melville Heritage Organization, is someone Joe and I have worked with over the years on other book projects. Before I had even decided to write another ghost book, Gloria had asked us to conduct an investigation at both the Brewster House and the Thompson House in Setauket, which also appears in this book.

As Joe and I walked through the house, Joe sensed a tremendous amount of spiritual energy, including those of British soldiers.

Orbs in the attic.

After we toured the first floor, we made our way up to the second floor. I was hoping to get some orb photos up there. For the first five minutes or so, neither I nor Joe captured anything. I knew the spirits were up there because I could sense them. I politely asked them if they could make their presence known through orbs. Within a minute, we both were capturing an abundance of orbs. In each photo, the orbs had moved around the frame. We kept shooting, and all of a sudden, as quick as they had come, is as quick as they had left. We went from having tons of orbs to nothing at all. We thanked the spirits for the gift of their presence, which added validity to our investigation.

Next, we did a question-and-answer segment using our recorders to detect both white noise EVPs and ghost box recordings. The white noise session did not reveal any EVPs. The house was very quiet, with little to no white noise, so this could have been the reason we didn't receive that type of EVP. Our ghost box recording session yielded numerous answers, and were recorded on the first floor of the house in the main kitchen area. We connected with three spirits. One was Robert, who could have possibly been Robert Townsend from the Culper Spy Ring; Caleb Brewster; and a man named

Kenneth Barton, who we could not identify. He did have a British accent, so it is possible that he was a British soldier who had visited the house.

Here is the transcript from the ghost box session:

> *Joe: So, is there anything you want to tell us about this house as we walk around?*
> *Spirit: Wounded. They all dead. Dead.*
> *Spirit: Got it?*
> *Joe: Got it.*
> *Spirit: Thank you!*
> *Joe: This is where the British sat?*
> *Spirit: They are not countrymen.*
> *Spirit: They were left for dead.*
> *Joe: We're using the ghost box. Play with the scanner.*
> *Spirit: Hello.*
> *Joe: My name is Joe. What's your name?*
> *Spirit: Robert.*
> *Joe: Robert?*
> *Spirit: In person.*
> *Joe: Is anyone from the Brewster family here?*
> *Spirit: Yes. Let me type…Kenneth Barton.* [Strong English accent!]
> *Joe: Is Caleb Brewster here?*
> *Spirit: Present.*
> *Joe: Amazing orbs upstairs in the attic of the Brewster house.*
> *Spirit: We know.*
> *Joe: We're done, yeah.*
> *Spirit: Thank God we're done!*
> *Joe: Thank God? Hahaha. Was it that painful?*
> *Spirit: No.*
> *Spirit: Caleb here. Caleb!*
> *Spirit: He faced many men.*
> *Joe: Anybody else have fun?*
> *Spirit: You and Kerriann.*
> *Spirit: Caleb lives at his spirit.*

Having the communication throughout our investigation was truly amazing. It was like stepping back in time, if only for a short while. We were happy to report back to the Ward Melville Heritage Organization that the Brewsters, Davises and spirits from the Revolutionary War live on.

Another interesting point to note is that a copy of genre painter William Sidney Mount's *Long Island Farmhouses*, in which the Brewster house is featured, is on display. When the Brewster house was restored in 1968, it was restored to match the 1845 painting.

If you have not yet been to the Brewster house, I suggest you make a trip. Be sure to call WMHO ahead of your visit to find out when it is open.

The Brewster house was listed in the National Register of Historic Places on February 28, 2008. In 2014, an archeological dig took place at the Brewster House, and most of the items found were shards of light ceramics, pearlware and whiteware from the eighteenth century. The Ward Melville Heritage Organization continues the upkeep on the building and grounds, while also running an on-site history program centering on George Washington's spy ring and its connection to Long Island.

3

MEADOW CROFT

SAYVILLE

T ucked away on sixty-four acres, surrounded by woods and marshlands, is a timeless piece of history known as Meadow Croft. As you turn onto a long dirt road off Middle Road in the village of Sayville, you will be surrounded by tall marsh grasses that flank the Brown's River. This peaceful and bucolic road leads you to a large colonial revival–style residence built in 1891. If the walls of Meadow Croft could talk, they would tell the story of a family with all their love, glory, tragedy and scandal. They would tell the story of the Roosevelts.

In the summer of 1873, Robert Barnwell Roosevelt, uncle to President Theodore Roosevelt, purchased 215 acres of land to the north of where Meadow Croft sits today, on the borderline of Sayville and Bayport. He built a summer home and named it Lotus Lake after two lakes that could be found on the property. The estate was a functioning farm and had been known as the David Lane Farm. Also on the property was a trout preserve, which Robert stocked himself. The house was demolished in 1958, and the original entrance to the estate is now Lotus Road, which is off McConnell Avenue.

Robert Barnwell Roosevelt was a lawyer, member of Congress, diplomat, politician, editor, author, conservationist and popular public speaker, among other things. He was also an avid sportsman and fly-fisherman. In 1850, he married Elizabeth "Lizzie" Thorne Ellis, and they lived in a house in New York City. They had four children together, John Ellis, Robert Barnwell Jr., Margaret and Helen, who died in childhood. Lizzie

Roosevelt died in 1887 at the age of fifty-seven-years old. Robert Sr.'s children, who were first cousins to Teddy Roosevelt, grew up spending their summers at Lotus Lake.

A year after his wife died, in 1888, Robert married Minnie O'Shea, from County Tipperary in Ireland. Robert had always been known as a "ladies man." What many people did not know, however, was that he led a double life during his marriage to Lizzie. For many years, his mistress was Minnie O'Shea, and Robert went as far as setting Minnie up in a house in New York City that was right down the street from where he lived with Lizzie. He told Minnie to assume the name Mrs. Robert Fortescue so that no one would find out about the affair. Together they had four children, one who died at a young age. After Lizzie died, Robert claimed to have fallen in love with Mrs. Fortescue, a widow. When they got married, he referred to the children as his stepchildren, when they were really his own. Minnie died in 1902.

In 1903, President Theodore Roosevelt made a trip out to the estate and came on horseback from Oyster Bay in the middle of the night so he would not be seen. It took him a little under four hours, and he traveled thirty-five miles. He arrived shortly before six o'clock in the morning. He had lunch at Meadow Croft and dinner at Lotus Lake. The president's secret service men did not know where he was, and when they found out, they took a night train out to Sayville. During his time at Lotus Lake, Robert and Teddy did not talk politics because Robert was a Democrat and President Roosevelt a Republican. In fact, in 1904, when Teddy was running for reelection, Robert refused the Democrat's designation for presidential elector to avoid embarrassing his nephew.

On June 14, 1906, Robert Barnwell Roosevelt died at Lotus Lake at seventy-seven years old, and he is buried in the family plot in the Green-Wood Cemetery in Brooklyn.

In 1890, Robert's son John Ellis Roosevelt purchased forty-five acres of land along with a farmhouse from Benjamin and Annie Woodward. The property was adjacent to Lotus Lake. He built his summer home from the existing farmhouse in 1891 and called it "Meadow Croft." He bought an additional thirty acres from his father for one dollar, bringing his total acreage to seventy-five acres. He commissioned well-known architect Isaac Green, a major landholder and prominent citizen of Sayville, to attach an estate mansion to the older mid-nineteenth-century Woodward farmhouse. The original farmhouse was renovated and converted into a service wing and is located toward the back of the house. The front addition, which faces south, was turned into a roomy colonial revival/Queen Anne–style

Meadow Croft.

residence where John Ellis Roosevelt would spend his summers until his death in 1939.

The elaborate façade of the house is dominated by a large porch and a central porte cochere. The interior of the house has a traditional great center hall plan, flanked by two rooms on either side—a formal dining room on the left and a large ladies' parlor on the right, which contains a piano made by Horace Waters and is original to the house. During the restoration of the house, the Roosevelt family donated the piano back, and the dimples in the floor matched exactly where the piano had sat for many years. The first floor of the house has been restored to look the way it did in 1910, with the exception of the library.

Back to the great hall, one of the nicest features in this room is a cozy inglenook, which contains a fireplace and built-in benches and is located under the massive staircase. The inglenook was a common architectural feature of that time period. As you go up the stairs from the great hall to the second floor, you might notice that one of the spindles on the railing is upside down. Boss Strong, the builder, claimed that as his trademark, stating, "Only God made things that were perfect." Also noteworthy in the great hall are two sets of beautiful Dutch doors that were used for cross ventilation and to keep animals out. There are other interesting features in the great hall, including two black wrought iron wall lights original to the home, annunciator call buttons for the servants, a lift elevator and a wonderful photo of John Ellis and his daughter Jean.

In the older part of the house, there is the library, which is now used as an orientation and display case, Mr. Roosevelt's workshop, the butler's pantry, a kitchen with original stove, icebox and ice chest, a servants' dining room and a laundry room. Upstairs there are several bedrooms and guest rooms, a nursery, the master bedroom, Mr. Roosevelt's dressing room and servants' quarters with a communal bathroom. Two cantilevered bathrooms were added on to the second floor for the family in 1909. The house was originally lit by gas, and a number of gas fixtures can still be seen throughout the house. There is also a third floor, which contains two more guest rooms and a sitting room. They were originally additional servant's quarters, but over time, they became the prized guest bedrooms because of the wonderful view of the bay they offered.

The household had a staff of approximately fifteen servants, which included a chauffeur. They did not have a butler. Some of the staff came from the Roosevelts' home in the city, while others were local people who might not have lived at the estate. The Roosevelt family would spend June through November at Meadow Croft, and on occasion, they would come out during the winter months.

John Ellis Roosevelt was born in New York City in 1853 and was called Jack by his family. He graduated from Columbia School of Law in 1874 and went on to become a prominent lawyer in the law firm Roosevelt and Kobbe. A Democrat like his father, he never ran for political office, but he did always support his cousin Teddy in his political ventures. John was a nature lover, a sportsman, an avid sailor and an artist.

He married Nannie Mitchell Vance on February 19, 1879, and they had three daughters—Anita Blanche (Pansy), Gladys and the youngest daughter, Eugenia (Jean), who was born on July 15, 1891, during the Roosevelts' first summer at Meadow Croft. In 1901, the year Theodore became the twenty-sixth president of the United States, John's daughter Pansy, at age twenty, became institutionalized for schizophrenia. She died in a Flushing institution in 1929 at forty-eight years old.

Gladys, the second daughter of John and Nannie, was socially prominent and had gained recognition as a painter. She was also a very skilled and avid horseback rider. She lived at Apple Tree Hill in Glen Head with her husband, Fairman Rogers Dick, and they did not have any children. In 1926, at the age of thirty-seven, Gladys was killed in a riding accident while taking a dangerous jump during a hunt at the Meadowbrook Club where she and her husband were members. Gladys is buried at the Roosevelt family plot in Brooklyn, and her tombstone reads, "Killed in the hunting field, November 3, 1926. A gallant life and a gallant death."

The youngest daughter, Jean, lived a long and prosperous life, and she was the last remaining Roosevelt to own Meadow Croft, the place where she was born. She was very interested in horticulture, and she was a connoisseur and collector of art. She was also a traveler and spent a one-year honeymoon traveling around the world with her husband, Philip J. Roosevelt, who was her second cousin. Jean and Philip had three children, Phillipa, P. James and John E. Roosevelt II. During her father's old age, it was Jean who took care of him. Although her primary residence was in Oyster Bay, Jean still came out to Meadow Croft quite often during the summer. She held onto the estate after her father's death, and she kept it until 1973, when it was acquired by Suffolk County. Jean died on May 13, 1984, at her home in Oyster Bay at the age of ninety-two.

John Ellis Roosevelt enjoyed a wonderful family life and marriage to Nannie Vance. Unfortunately, in 1912, both John and Nannie contracted typhoid fever during their time at Meadow Croft. John recovered, but Nannie did not. After thirty-three years of marriage, Nannie passed away at Meadow Croft at fifty-two years old.

Some say that John Ellis was on the rebound when he married his brother's divorced sister-in-law, Edith Hammersley Biscoe, just two years later in 1914. Edith was twenty-nine years old, and John was sixty-one. Needless to say, the marriage lasted only a year, with divorce proceedings beginning in 1915 and the decree finalized in 1916.

John Ellis died in Delray Beach, Florida, on March 9, 1939, at the age of eighty-six. Not much is known about John Ellis's sister Margaret, but his younger brother, Robert Barnwell II (known to the family as Bert), lived on the northern part of the Roosevelt property, where he built a house called The Lilacs. Robert Jr.'s life was not without tragedy either. He married Grace Woodhouse in 1890, and they had one daughter together named Olga. Grace died four years later, in 1894. In 1898, Robert married Lilie Hamersley of Bayport, and they had two children, Robert B. Roosevelt III, who was born in 1899, the same year The Lilacs was built, and Lilie, born in 1907. In April 1922, at age twenty-three, Robert III was killed in New York City when he fell in front of a taxi and then was run over by a bus and killed. He became the first Roosevelt to be buried in St. Ann's Cemetery in Sayville.

By 1910, the entire Roosevelt compound consisted of 250 acres. The Lilacs, like Lotus Lake, was demolished in the late 1950s, leaving Meadow Croft the only home left on what is now sixty-four acres.

Other outbuildings still existing on the estate today include a carriage house, the auto house, an in-ground pool, which is one of the earliest intact swimming pools in the area, a shed, which was used as John Ellis Roosevelt's art studio (he later moved it to the upstairs of the carriage house) and a caretaker's cottage. A stable and pig barn were once located behind the carriage house, but they were in disrepair and collapsed. There were additional outbuildings during the Roosevelts' stay at Meadow Croft, but it is said that Mrs. Roosevelt had them torn down when she got tired of paying taxes on unused buildings.

During the spring and summer, a formal garden is maintained by volunteer members of the Bayport–Blue Point Heritage Association, and a vegetable garden is maintained by the Sayville Garden Club, which donates the produce to the Sayville Pantry.

In the 1950s, Jean Roosevelt sold fifteen acres of land at the back end of the estate to Bernard "Barney" Loughlin. Barney's parents, Michael and Mary, were caretakers at Meadow Croft, and they also oversaw the property when the Roosevelts were away and during the winter months. Their son, Barney, was born on the John Ellis Roosevelt estate in 1925, and after serving in World War II, Barney came back to Meadow Croft and became the caretaker, following in his parents' footsteps. He married Christine Benderoth in 1946, and they had three daughters. Barney and his family had moved off the estate but lived only a few blocks away. After the war, Barney had built a linotype shop on the Roosevelt property, which he eventually moved to Railroad Avenue.

During the 1970s, Meadow Croft fell into disrepair. Both Barney and Jean knew the important historical significance of the property and set out to preserve it. It was actually Barney Loughlin who approached the county to help restore it.

In 1984, Barney, along with his wife and daughters, decided to plant grapevines. The locals told him he could not possibly grow grapes on the South Shore, so he set out to prove them wrong. The grapes grew, and he sold them to vineyards out east. Eventually, he decided to produce his own wine, and he built his own winery called Loughlin Vineyards in the late 2000s. Barney passed away in 2017 at the age of ninety-one. His daughters still maintain the vineyard and winery, which is located on the property directly behind Meadow Croft. It is open to the public.

Suffolk County purchased Meadow Croft and the remaining sixty-four acres in 1974, and the house was added to the National Register of Historic Places in 1987. The care and restoration of the house and property is shared with the Bayport–Blue Point Heritage Organization, which first envisioned its potential as a museum in 1984. Meadow Croft is open for tours June through October.

Joe and I pulled down the long dirt driveway to the estate where we were meeting Richard Martin, the director of historic services for Suffolk County; Leanne Berg, vice president of the Bayport–Blue Point Heritage Organization; and Frank Giebfried, a board member and docent at Meadow Croft. We walked along the massive front porch and through the Dutch doors into the great hall, where so many of the Roosevelts had once gathered. Before our tour of the house, we settled in the old farmhouse area, which is now the library, and interviewed Richard, Leanne and Frank.

Richard began by telling us about the South Shore Roosevelts' connection to Theodore Roosevelt and shared some more interesting facts with us.

"John Ellis Roosevelt and Theodore Roosevelt actually grew up together in neighboring town houses in Manhattan," Richard began. "As cousins, they were very close. They were childhood friends and their backyards joined each other. Then later in life, in their teenage years, they stayed friends and actually went hunting together on occasion."

As for Robert Barnwell Roosevelt and his family, Richard said, "It was a family compound with all adjoining properties. They all really appreciated this south shore environment for the activities here. They all sailed, they went hunting, fishing, and this was really a wildlife paradise at that time." He continued, "This house was a fairly modest house, considering the size of the houses built back then, and it was considered a summer house. They did visit in the winter. We have sleighs in the carriage house, so they came out for sleigh riding during the winter on occasion."

Richard then went on to explain that after John Ellis married his second wife, the entire inside of the house had been whitewashed while they were on their honeymoon.

"Everything was painted white," said Richard. "So that was a real transition time from the first wife to the second wife. Everything you see here, all the natural wood, was painted. So, when the county maintenance painters did the work in the late '80s and early '90s, they really had their work cut out for them. Then in 1983, the Bayport–Blue Point Heritage Organization started fundraising, and that's when things really started."

We talked a while more about the history of Meadow Croft and how some of the furnishings, including the piano, are original pieces that were returned either from Barney Loughlin or from the Roosevelt family.

Our discussion then shifted to ghosts. Richard, a nonbeliever, turned to Leanne, who shared her stories with us.

"We're here all the time, cleaning or reorganizing," said Leanne. "And you can hear voices…conversations. Sometimes you can hear music or sounds. I've had my hair brushed. There's been a lot of things, for me anyway. My son [age seventeen at the time] has come in here and has said to me, 'Do you hear the conversations?' and I'll stop and listen and say, 'I do.'"

"People always ask us if we have ghosts," added Frank. "I have not really experienced anything, just a little voice here or there, but nothing that I would attribute to anything supernatural. I'm a skeptic, but I'm not going to not believe the things people tell me they experience."

"I see shadows at times," continued Leanne, "but sometimes I wonder if that's just in my own head."

"Have you ever heard footsteps?" asked Joe.

"Yes, as a matter of fact," said Leanne. "We had a board meeting here just the other night, and everybody was talking. My father is also on the board, and he was sitting next to me, and he kind of just tapped me, and I said, 'I know. I hear it.' When I first started working with our president, she always said, 'I've never heard anything. I want to hear something.' Then one day she did, and she said, 'I don't know if I really want to hear this.' But every so often she will hear something and will ask me if I heard it.

"The music I've heard comes from upstairs. It sounds like a record is playing on the old Victrola, but obviously, it was not the Victrola."

As we were discussing this, Joe saw a figure walk past the window. He said it was a light shadow.

"For me, I've seen a black shadow and a light shadow out of the corner of my eye. I associate the light colored shadow as female." said Leanne. "There is also a dog, I believe. I almost tripped over it one night when I went into a dark room and realized, 'Oh my gosh! There's a dog in here!' Then I saw the shadow of the dog on the floor."

After our interviews, we walked around the house. Joe had an overall feeling that the servants enjoyed working for the Roosevelts and that the female energy in the house was quite strong, proud and self-assured.

"When we set up for our interview, I immediately saw the figure of a man outside pass by the front window through the doorframe of the adjacent room," said Joe. "I did feel like lots of people in spirit were running about

Inglenook fireplace in the great hall, where Joe captured orbs on his video camera.

while the interview proceeded. I feel this was more of the imprinted energy from the past. Servants preparing for dinner and parties, guests arriving."

Joe had been taking video throughout our tour. During our walk through the great hall, Joe captured a large amount of orb activity by the inglenook fireplace. As for me, I picked up activity on the ghost meter while talking to Frank in front of the servants' staircase in the older part of the house. I was holding the meter while I was talking with Frank, and it was on. All of a sudden, for no apparent reason, it went off with a fast-paced progression of beeps, and then it stopped.

In the kitchen, Joe saw an orb fly past from right to left. At the same time, I had commented how the room became instantly cold. More orbs were seen by Joe near a photo of Gladys, by the third-floor stairway and in the nursery. While we were upstairs, after we had just left the kitchen, Joe heard the sound of men's voices coming up the staircase. Leanne went to check and see if someone had just come into the house, but when she did, no one was there. Footsteps had also been heard coming from the third floor.

As for my photographs, while I was standing in the great hall, I captured two fleeting orbs through the doorway of the parlor, above and below the piano. Also, in the great hall I took an overall shot of the room toward the back end so you could see the front entrance door. From where I was

The servants' staircase in the older part of the house, where the ghost meter picked up activity.

standing, the large photo of John Ellis and Jean would be to the right of the Dutch door. In front of the photo was another fleeting orb. Unfortunately, neither of the orb photos would have produced well in the book since they were fleeting and slightly out of focus.

We decided to conduct our ghost box recordings in the great hall in front of the inglenook. Here is our communication:

> *Joe: Are the Roosevelts here?*
> *Spirit: They're not dead!*
> *Kerriann: How many of you are here with us today?*
> *Spirit: Counting private residents, per se?*
> *Staff: Do you like what we're doing here?*
> *Spirit: Uh-huh.*
> *Kerriann: Uh-huh. Did you hear that?*
> *Spirit: You're on track.*
> *Joe: We love you!*
> *Spirit: Cool!*
> *Staff: Are any of the Roosevelt daughters here with us?*
> *Spirit: Some.*
> *Kerriann: Some.*

Kerriann: Are you happy this is going into a book?
Spirit: It will take off.
Kerriann: John, are you here?
Spirit: Yes.
Joe: Yes.
Kerriann: Were you happy in your house?
Spirit: I've never been uncomfortable.
Kerriann: John, are you here in the house with us now?
Spirit: John.
Joe: John? Did you hear John? They just said, John.
Kerriann: I heard him, yes.
Spirit: John.
Staff: John, are we keeping up the history correctly?
Spirit: Comfortable.
Kerriann: It's comfortable.
Staff: Nannie, are you here?
Spirit: She's here.
Group: She's here! She's here!

According to the National Register of Historic Places, Meadow Croft is a rare example of that transitional stage of Long Island history in which the agricultural and farming texture of the region was first giving way to resort and estate development. It is the sole surviving South Shore homestead of the family and the most tangible symbol of the Roosevelt family's presence in southeast Long Island.

Luckily, it can now be enjoyed for generations to come.

4

FARM COUNTRY KITCHEN

RIVERHEAD

The fifteen-mile Peconic River is the longest river on Long Island, and it runs through the Central Long Island Pine Barrens. The mouth of this shallow river is Peconic Bay, just east of Riverhead, which was founded in 1792. The river serves as a border between Brookhaven and Riverhead. It is primarily a freshwater river, until it runs into Riverhead, where it becomes an estuary. It is here that Riverhead got its name.

The river water powered many important businesses in the 1800s, including several sawmills, gristmills, a paper mill, a woolen mill and a flour mill, among others. The freshwater areas served the ice harvesting industry, while the surrounding acidic marshes, bogs and wetlands made it an ideal habitat for growing cranberries. A 165-acre park, known today as the Cranberry Bog Preserve County Park (located on the west side of Lake Avenue), loops around Sweezy Pond, which was created in the late 1800s to flood the cranberry bog. The cranberry industry in Riverhead ran from 1875 to 1930.

Riverhead was also the home to many farmers and growers, harness makers, cigar makers, carpenters and later, shipbuilders. The oldest continuous business, which was started in 1842 by George Hill, was a monument business that created hundreds of gravestones for area residents. Today, the business still exists and is known as the Peconic Monument Works.

Many businesses and several homes were located on West Main Street in Riverhead, and a map of the area from 1909 shows familiar names like Griffing, Sweezy (an important figure in the ice industry) and Hill. Today,

West Main Street comprises several businesses and a few residential homes. Many of the old homes that still exist are now used for business purposes. One of them is Farm Country Kitchen.

Located along the Peconic River between Marcy Avenue and Sweezy Avenue, this delightful eatery is tucked away on a picturesque piece of land and has become a well-known dining hot spot in Riverhead. The building was once the home of Lester Hill, who more than likely was connected to the monument builders. On either side of the house was the home of William Sweezy and Mary Higgins. The building is believed to have been built in the early 1800s. Besides the 1909 map listing the names of the property owners, there were no other historical records I could come up with that would give the exact date the house was built or its occupants over the years. We did find out a few things from Farm Country Kitchen owner Tom Carson on the day Joe and I went there to interview him.

Tom purchased the house and property, which sits on 0.75 acres, in 2002. He also purchased the two properties on either side of the restaurant, the old Sweezy house and the Higgins house, which he plans to renovate. Before it became Farm Country Kitchen, two landscape architects owned and worked out of the house, and one lived there. They both passed away, and the house was left to a friend who settled the estate.

Tom Carson had bought his first restaurant when he was twenty-five years old. His degree is actually in computer science with a minor in accounting. He quickly grew tired of the industry and decided to buy a restaurant with a friend of his in Port Jefferson. He did that for two years and then he married his wife, Maria; sold the business; and took some time off from the culinary world. After his children were born, he started making salads out of his house. His wife, whose family owns a restaurant in Mount Sinai, worked with him in the early years and sold the salads to the community.

"I started the business from scratch," said Tom. "It was hard, really hard, but I'm glad I did it. I needed to find a place for the business, and I didn't want to pay rent on a store. There was a building down by the aquarium, and it was perfect, and then the deal fell through. Then somebody mentioned this house was for sale."

He continued, "This house was not presentable. The house next door was boarded up. There was an old diner, there was a trailer; across the street was an old transmission building, which was dilapidated looking. When I saw this house, it was boarded up. I saw the river. I saw the potential of my own business. It was January. It was terrible in here. The roof was leaking, and I said, 'I'll take it.' I gave the girl a hundred bucks, and that's how I got started."

Tom Carson started his business on the first anniversary of September 11, and since then, business has grown one-hundred-fold.

"The house is over two hundred years old. Many families have lived here," Tom continued. "I have people coming in off the streets telling me about this place. There was a local judge. He grew up in this town. He's seventy-five now, and he used to play here as a kid. This was a working river. There was a cranberry bog. Eventually, the town tried to improve certain areas and zoned it for business."

Farm Country Kitchen is a major attraction in Riverhead, with people going there before and after shopping at the outlets, which are located down the road. The restaurant has even seen the likes of Hollywood celebrities, professional athletes and TV personalities. The food is farm to table, with an eclectic menu offering all fresh items that are made on the premises, and everything, including sauces, are made from scratch.

"People know us as a really neat, creative food place in this quirky, old, shabby chic house," said Tom. "It draws a certain personality. We get people who want to venture out for something different."

The old house had to be completely renovated when Tom purchased it. It needed new walls, moldings, flooring, a new roof, plumbing, electric, new sidewalks and landscaping. Today, the restaurant seats fifty inside,

Farm Country Kitchen.

and during the summer, another twenty-five to thirty people can be seated outside along the river. The views from most of the tables in the restaurant are beautiful. Upstairs there is also a small room for private parties.

After learning about the restaurant, our conversation with Tom quickly changed to the paranormal:

> *I came to this place completely unaware of anything. I'd be here at 4:00 a.m. sometimes, by myself, and start the kitchen up. I'd make the soups. I did everything myself in the beginning. I'd be upstairs in my office doing something, and I'd hear the door close downstairs. I'm not kidding. Or I'd be down here and I'd hear footsteps upstairs and I would be frozen in my tracks. And I'm thinking, what's going on here? Is it the wind outside or something? I'd look and there would be nobody. It would happen on many occasions. I'd hear noises, and doors closing in this house. Just last week I was upstairs. I had just come back from vacation, and I heard the door close. And I'm like, oh, the boys are coming in to work. Then I come downstairs and there's nobody here. I looked outside and no one was there. I thought maybe someone was coming and was knocking on the door. So I'm thinking, that was weird, and I didn't think that it was a ghost or spirit. I was thinking it's just, whatever, and that I'm imagining things.*

Tom continued, "There have been many times before where I've heard noises upstairs and I go upstairs, and I look around. How does that happen? But as time went on, I began to realize this house has good bones, and I say this house has good ghosts because there is positive karma here. Customers are happy when they come here. Everyone calls this place a little gem. I truly believe this house has been blessed. We were drawn here."

We were all seated in the little dining area in the front of the house, which faces the street. Tom revealed to us that just the day before a woman came into that room and started talking about the spirits.

"Yesterday afternoon there was a woman sitting and having lunch here," said Tom. "She says to the waiter, 'There are spirits in this house.' So, the waiter came up to me and said the lady over there thinks there are spirits and ghosts here. I said, 'There are!' I went over to her and said, 'Hi, I'm Tom. You feel there are spirits here?' and she said yes. I said, 'I do too.' I told her my story of hearing noises upstairs, and doors closing. So she took a picture yesterday afternoon of her children against the wall here," Tom pointed to the area. "They were a family of four. And there was no sun, and they were eating lunch in this room in the corner where there is

The staircase where a customer saw a ghostly woman feeding her baby.

no extra light. And it was dark and gray and raining yesterday. She took the picture, and above the window there was a big glare of white covering the window. It was just another sign that this house is alive with the people who loved it."

The stories did not end there.

"We had a woman here once, about ten years ago, who was standing at the base of the stairs, and she said that she saw a woman feeding her baby at the top of the stairs. You can't make something like that up!" said Tom. "I've experienced the most because I'm always here alone. I'm here before everybody. I hear the noises and the shuffling. I've never seen anything though."

Several employees have also claimed to hear noises upstairs. The upstairs rooms seem to have the most energy. Tom admits that he never really feels alone when he is working up there.

During our walk around the restaurant, Joe commented that he felt nothing but good energy there, and he sensed the presence of both male and female spirits upstairs in the private dining room. As I made my way around, I took lots of photographs with two cameras. At one point, I was

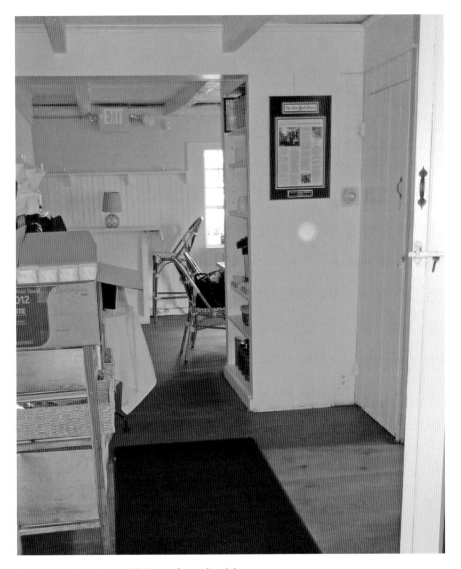

Orb captured on the wall below a framed article.

standing in the main dining area in the back of the restaurant, where I was photographing the hall that leads to the smaller dining room in the front of the restaurant. On a wall very near the staircase to go upstairs, I captured an orb. I had taken several shots in this area standing in the same spot, and only in the one image did the orb appear.

Our most successful connection that day came during our ghost box session, which was quite extensive. Our recording ran over eleven minutes, and Tom and Maria were absolutely amazed at what was coming through. Along with spirits who might have been connected to the house, we also communicated with some of the Carsons' family members and friends, including possibly Tom's father.

In one question I asked if anyone died in the house. The spirit replied loudly, "Norma." Joe then did a number counting session where Joe says "one" and then the spirits reply in sequence. The spirits replied, "It's three, four and five, six, seven and eight."

Kerriann: Do you like that we can use the box to communicate?
Spirit: In general, it's okay for whatever.
Kerriann: You can communicate with us through this.
Spirit: In the farmer's kitchen?
Kerriann: We want to write a good story about this restaurant.
Spirit: Hello.
Kerriann: Are you happy this story is going into a book?
Spirit: Where?
Spirit: No.
Joe: Spirits, you have to interrupt the scan…
Spirit: I did.
Joe: …and blank out the noise so we can hear your voice.
Spirit: Got it.
Joe: Got it.
Tom: Does Tom have anything to say?
Spirit: Tom.
Joe: This is his Dad.
Spirit: Don't complicate.
Tom: Does he have anything to say to me?
Spirit: Eight! [Continuing the number count]
Spirit: Set your vision.
Joe: Repeat it again, spirits.
Spirit: I'll text you.
Group: I'll text you!
Joe: Is Tom's dad here?
Spirit: Tom's higher.
Joe: I think he said he's higher.

Spirit: Grace he knew.
Spirit: I like balloons.
Tom: Can you tell the spirits, do me a favor?
And have them stop breaking things.
So, when things go to the floor, they don't break?
Spirit: She's not breaking!

In yet another session I had asked if there were a lot of spirits who visited here. The spirit replied, "Yes." This next session was taken up in Tom's office, and the spirits told us how many guests were in the restaurant at the time of our visit. Tom immediately ran down the stairs and did a head count. The spirits were off by one. Here is how that session went:

Tom: Are there too many people here?
Spirit: Twenty.
Group: Twenty.
Joe: Could you do a count? [At this point Tom ran down the stairs
    to count.]
Maria: That one I heard clearly.
Joe: Yeah.
Joe: You guys loved him, don't you? [A reference to a family friend.]
Spirit: Nice.
Kerriann: Are you happy we are including this in the book?
Spirit: Yes.
Joe: I think I heard a yes there.
[Tom comes back up the stairs.]
Tom: Nineteen customers here.
Spirit: Yes.
Group: Oh my God!

This is just a sampling of the wonderful ghost box EVPs we received that day. We were all grateful for the communication, and we made believers out of Tom and Maria. Not only did it give them confirmation to the continuity of life, but it also gave them reassurance that their loved ones continue to be there for them from the other side. It also confirmed the good energy that seems to abound at Farm Country Kitchen.

"People thought I was crazy buying this property," said Tom. "I had no plan. My wife said to me, 'Don't worry about it. You'll figure it out.' When you do something from scratch, you never think it's going to become anything. And every single day I've been here, from the beginning, something positive happens. Like today, you guys are here.

"It's a pretty neat place, I must say," continued Tom. "I love my life, and I love this place. I never get tired of coming here."

5

SMITH ESTATE AT LONGWOOD

RIDGE

Longwood, as it is most commonly known, is located on thirty-five acres in Ridge and has been preserved and maintained by the Town of Brookhaven since 1975. The house is part of a historic manor built in the late eighteenth century, and it was altered and enlarged during the nineteenth century. The land on which the manor sits was part of a huge parcel of wild land that was purchased from the Indians by Colonel William "Tangier" Smith in 1691, as the Manor of St. George.

Colonel Smith was British and had been living in Tangier, Africa, where he had become mayor. After the British evacuation of the city, Smith came to America. Because of Smith's service in Tangier, along with being a man of means, he was allowed to purchase a large tract of land on the south side of Long Island. The Manor of St. George was approximately 40 percent of the current Brookhaven Town. Smith leased a portion of the land to the Indians with whom he coexisted peacefully. In 1693, Governor Benjamin Fletcher, through a patent, elevated the land status to manor. Additional land patents were given to Smith in 1697 and extended from Southampton to Southold.

William "Tangier" Smith built his home on the northern section, at the time called Smith's Neck. The house at Mastic was built later, but there is no record of William Tangier and his wife living there. The northern section of the larger purchase was referred to as the "swamp" or "longswamp" and is the area where Longwood would eventually be built. It was bound by the Carman's River and the Forge River, previously known as the Connecticut River or the Mastic River.

Smith became active in local government, where he held many positions, including commander of the Suffolk County Militia, where he was given the title of colonel. He died circa 1705 at the age of fifty-seven, and he left behind a wife and six children, who became the heirs to Long Island's largest estate. According to the tradition of the day, neither Smith's wife nor his three daughters could inherit the property, so instead, it was divided three ways among his sons. Smith's oldest son, Colonel Henry Smith, inherited the northern tract of land, which was bound by Long Island Sound. The other two sons, Major William Henry Smith and Charles Jeffrey Smith, acquired the land on the southern side of the island. Charles Jeffrey Smith died of smallpox in 1715 at the age of twenty-one. He was unmarried, so his inheritance was divided among surviving family members.

During the Revolutionary War, the "swamp" was used for farming, woodcutting and pasturing livestock, and the pond located behind the Longwood estate might have been used as a watering hole. As for the manor house in Mastic, it was taken over and occupied by the British and renamed Fort St. George.

Judge William Smith, grandson of William Tangier Smith, was anti-British and did not live at the manor at the time of the Revolution. Some accounts state that he might have taken refuge at the "swamp," where he moved his livestock to protect them from British confiscation. Judge Smith had several children, and after the war, he had a house built at the "swamp" for his son General John Smith. Long Swamp, as it was called at the time, was built circa 1790. The original part of the house was built very similarly to the manor house. It was a large Georgian home with a center hall and two square rooms on each side, each with corner fireplaces. A kitchen was located on the eastern wing of the house. Unfortunately, John's wife died before they moved into the house, and John decided to remain in Mastic. His father, Judge Smith, then gave the house to his second son, William Smith, who moved in with his wife, Hannah.

Between 1792 and 1799, William and Hannah had five children. Their first daughter, Phoebe, died during infancy, and a terrible tragedy occurred with their fifth child, Betsy. Hannah learned that her father had died just before Christmas in 1799. He had been living in Smithtown, and despite the fact that Hannah was pregnant, she traveled by horse and carriage to the funeral. During her stay there, she gave birth on Christmas day to Betsy. Hannah and Betsy stayed in Smithtown until a few days after the new year and then they set out to go back home to Long Swamp. The roads were icy, and while traveling through Middle Island, their carriage overturned, and

Betsy was killed. Hannah was not seriously injured, but she never recovered from the death of both her father and her child. She died of a broken heart in the fall of 1800.

William, now a widower, had to take care of the remaining three children. Less than two years after Hannah passed, William died, leaving the children orphans. For a short time, they went to live with General John Smith at the manor house. Long Swamp was now left without a proprietor. John decided to send his own son William to live at Long Swamp and manage the farm there until Hannah and William's child William Sidney was old enough to run the house and farm. On his twenty-first birthday, July 8, 1817, William Sidney Smith left his job in New York and came back to his birth home at Long Swamp, where he became the sole proprietor of the estate. He decided to change the name of the estate from Long Swamp to Longwood.

William, a bachelor, lived alone at the house for about six months and then moved into the Manor of St. George. It wasn't until he married Eleanor Jones from Cold Spring Harbor that he moved back into Longwood, where the couple lived with their three-year old son, William Henry. The year was 1824, and Longwood at this time was situated on seven thousand acres. The house had gone through some architectural changes and redecorating, the style being that of Gothic Revival.

Like his ancestors before him, William Sidney was very active in local government, while at the same time he managed the farm, and co-owned a sawmill, woolen mill and gristmill in Yaphank. He was a great businessman with extensive holding in mortgages and bonds, and he was an exceptional farmer. He leased other farmland, and he continued woodcutting contracts and livestock holdings. It is said that by 1860 the income from his farm alone was estimated at $7,300 per year. That was a huge amount of money for its day.

William Sidney and Eleanor were very happy at Longwood, and they ended up having ten children there. At times, William invited relatives and close friends to live with them at the estate as well. Longwood was a very active household with lots of children always running around. Because of this growing family, the house was enlarged once again sometime circa 1840–50. It was at this time that it was embellished and took on the Colonial Revival style, which included the front porches.

The children were raised in the house and grew up with governesses and tutors before they each went away to school. When they became adults, eight of the children moved away to various parts of the country, while two

Longwood Estate.

children, Robert Russell Smith and Amelia Smith, continued to live at home with their parents.

In 1873, William Sidney and Eleanor were married fifty years, and a huge celebration with over 150 people in attendance took place at Longwood. All ten children came back to their birth home with their own families, and an elaborate party took place. The celebration lasted for two days, and the Smiths could not have been happier. The gathering of family and friends was very important to them.

As time went on and the Smiths continued to age, Robert and Amelia started taking a more active role in running the estate and household. On January 19, 1879, the patriarch of the family, William Sidney, died at age eighty-three. Eleanor died five years later, on May 7, 1884, after a long illness. She was seventy-nine years old. Both William and Eleanor are buried at the Longwood family cemetery, along with about twenty-eight other family members.

After their deaths, things began to change at Longwood. Before he died, William had divided the estate into ten parcels consisting of approximately seven hundred acres each. A parcel was given to each of the nine children. The tenth parcel, which contained the house and twelve hundred acres, was given to Robert, since he was the first child born on the estate and the one who had taken care of the estate and his parents as they aged.

Robert married a woman by the name of Cornelia Thorne, and they had two children at Longwood, William Sidney Tangier Smith and Helen Tangier Smith. Unfortunately, Robert died in 1885. Cornelia moved away after the death of her husband, and Longwood was then used primarily as a summer estate.

By 1917, Camp Upton was constructed on ten thousand acres east of the Longwood estate. Camp Upton later became the Brookhaven National Laboratory, as we know it today. William S. Tangier studied at Columbia University and went on to become a doctor with a practice in Brooklyn. In 1918, he was also a captain in the Army Medical Corps. He died in 1944.

As for Helen Tangier Smith, she spent all of her summers at Longwood, and took an interest in her family's history. She spent a lot of time researching and organizing the information she came across, with the hopes that it would be preserved one day. Helen was the last of her line and never married. On her death in 1955, she had willed Longwood and 750 acres to her cousin Elbert Clayton Smith, who had been living with his family in California. He decided to move the family to Longwood after he inherited it. Along with taking care of the estate, he took on a job at the Brookhaven National Laboratory as a business manager, and a few years later, he started his own consulting company.

He loved Longwood and was very generous to the community. He decided to scale down the estate's acreage, so he donated fifty-one acres to the Board of Education for the building of Longwood High School, six acres went to the Middle Island Presbyterian Church, and two acres were divided between Suffolk County for the making of the greenbelt and to St. Mark's Lutheran Church.

Elbert had plans to continue the preservation of Longwood, but he died suddenly in 1967. His wife, Eleanor, moved back to California, and the house and property were sold to real estate developers Levitt and Company. A year later, in 1968, the contents of the house were sold at auction. Longwood's fate was unknown.

By 1973, Wilbur F. Breslin and Herbert Carmel had purchased the property and had plans to build a residential, industrial and commercial complex. Local residents, along with local government officials, fought to have Longwood preserved. In what was called a "generous gesture," Wilbur Breslin and Herbert Carmel had a change of heart and offered the house and thirty-five acres to the Town of Brookhaven in 1974. By 1981, the Smith Estate at Longwood was placed in the National Register of Historic Places and is continued to be preserved today.

Along with the house and family cemetery, the property contains several outbuildings, including a caretaker's cottage, an icehouse, a garage, a woodshed and carriage barns. The big brown barn on the property was brought to the estate after the original barn was burned down by vandals. Also on the property is a small-frame, one-room schoolhouse, which was moved to the estate in 1977.

Joe and I did our first investigation at Longwood back in the spring of 2017. Subsequently, Joe returned several other times with his paranormal group, many of whom experienced things in the house. Longwood has a plethora of activity, which makes sense because it was a very active and happy household for centuries.

Joe and I arrived at Longwood on a beautiful, sunny day, and met up with Longwood's director, Diane Schwindt. Diane has been the director at Longwood for over fifteen years. Her background is in horticulture, so she knew how to spin, weave and do things with plants. She began a garden on the property and started to run programs, including colonial school tours. Diane loves the house and has taken great pride in doing her share to preserve it. She has only felt good energy at Longwood.

So, on the day we arrived, Diane was outside doing some work around the garden near the woodshed and garage, not far from the house. We made our introductions, and as we approached the front porch of the house, Joe blurted out, "Who's the man in black?" Diane stopped dead in her tracks. Diane knew what Joe was referring to, because she had experienced the man in black too.

"When I first started working at Longwood, from the corner of my eye I would see a man dressed in black…tall. If I had to pick a period I would say 1800ish," said Diane. "I would see him out by the garage and icehouse. For years, he would be watching me, and every once and a while, I would be working in the front of the house and I would catch him over by the wheelchair ramp behind the tree…a silhouette, just for that split second. I have always been aware of his presence. He's a tall man in black. I just always knew he was there. There was only one occasion when I thought he was in the house. I actually saw a shadow walk through the hallway."

Diane was amazed that Joe, who she hadn't met prior, picked up on the man in black immediately.

"No way!" said Diane. "So, I wasn't seeing things."

Diane has experienced other phenomena in the house, including doors opening and closing, the scent of roses, the smell of cigarettes or a pipe and the musky smell of male body odor. She has also experienced items in the house being moved around.

"I am very particular about the house, and I always want everything to be perfect in case somebody walks in," said Diane. "When I saw the door moving, I got up and went into the front parlor. The candles were at a forty-five degree angle, and the grandfather clock door was open. It was at that same time that I smelled the overpowering scent of roses in the hallway."

When she first started doing school programs, Diane had a group of children in the front parlor, and she was talking about George Washington's Culper Spy Ring. Diane told us that the teacher was standing in the room with them taking a few photos. In one of the photos tons of orbs appeared.

"I could tell from the look on the teacher's face that she got something," Diane said.

Another common occurrence has been the sound of little children running through the house when nobody is there. Diane and other employees have heard it on several occasions. When Joe came back to Longwood with his group several months after we had been there, the sound of children's laughter could be heard, and Joe reported that the area upstairs that is currently set up as a child's room seems to have an abundance of spiritual energy. Other visitors claim they have heard the sound of little children running or falling down the stairs.

It is of no surprise that the energy of all the children who lived and played at Longwood has remained and has created this type of phenomenon. Diane and another employee have also heard their names being called very clearly when no one else is in the building.

"I definitely feel that whoever is here is very protective over the house," said Diane.

Joe and I conducted our interview with Diane in the front parlor. As we sat on a small couch facing Diane, we both could sense someone sitting in between us. After the interview, Joe and I started wandering around the rooms on the main floor. Joe went into the piano room, and a shadowy figured passed by the door.

"I sensed it was a man, not a woman," said Joe.

As we continued to make our way around the house, we experienced two different doors closing. We searched the room and immediately ruled out open windows. On entering the upstairs, Joe smelled the male body odor Diane spoke about in a small side room that contained an old shoe display.

Investigations Joe would conduct at Longwood at later dates revealed more phenomena such as the sound of footsteps, bangs and furniture moving around upstairs, as well as cold and hot spots and light anomalies.

Joe in the back Victorian parlor, where a shadowy figure passed by the door.

"I think the spirits like the house as a portal," said Joe, "not only historically, but also because the house acts as a giant vessel for communication due to the sheer size of the property and all the people and activities that have occurred there during its history."

During our walkthrough, Joe and I conducted three ghost box sessions that yielded over twenty audible responses from the spirits. More ghost box EVPs were recorded with Joe's group as well. In December 2017, Joe captured a voice on the ghost box saying, "1790," which as we know, is when the house was built. Almost a year later, Joe and a member of his group asked, "Do you know the girl who frequents here often?" The spirit responded, and Joe thought she said "Ellen," but the spirit replied, "Ellie." In May 2017, Joe and I also captured the voice of a female spirit outside of the house. The spirit said, "It's Ellie."

What's fascinating about these EVPs are the fact that twice, Ellie, short for Eleanor, came through. Could this be the spirit of Eleanor Smith?

In another exchange while working with the ghost box upstairs, I asked, "How many of you [spirits] are here?" We were standing in a small room where several colored glass bottles sat in a window. In answer to my question, a spirit replied, "Who are you?" Then Joe replied, "I'm Joe." Another spirit chimed in, saying, "Hello, it's Maryanne." Joe then apologized for not introducing ourselves. After that a spirit said, "I raised a nice property."

Joe in the shoe room listening for EVPs on the ghost box.

Continuing on with our questions, Joe asked, "Could you introduce yourselves? Give us your names?"

We then heard a spirit say, "I'm Alvin, the tall one," and another one said, "William." We believed at this point that we were communicating with three different spirits, one of them more than likely being one of the William Smiths. When we questioned them again, asking if there were three spirits communicating with us, another spirit voice responded, "A lot of them."

We had several ghost box EVPs that day. Here is a small sampling:

> *Kerriann: Do you remain here in the house?*
> *Joe: No, they're on the other side. Let me define that. So you've passed obviously?*
> *Spirit: The other side.*
> *Joe: On the other side. Did you hear them say the other side?*

In this next EVP, the spirits make reference to Joe and me using the ghost box:

Kerriann: Are you glad that we are here?
Spirit: Using the box.

Lastly, I believe we made communication with the man who was seen by both Joe and Diane, who may actually be one of the William Smiths. The clarity in this EVP was truly remarkable:

Kerriann: Who is the gentleman that's outside by the front porch?
Spirit: You're talking to him.

Through our time spent at Longwood, the one thing we surmised was that it was a place well loved, where family and friends gathered and where the spirits from the past like to come back and visit. Today, the house and property are used for school programs, handicap programs and events like the senior picnic, the boy scouts camping trip and the popular fall fair, which is always a favorite for the community.

As for Diane, she takes the ghosts in stride, realizing that they are just people from the past. She has great respect for them and the wonderful history they have left behind at Longwood. Diane has even been known to leave classical music playing for them when she is ready to lock up and go home.

"It's about respecting the past," said Diane. "That's what I love about here."

6

EARLE-WIGHTMAN HOUSE

OYSTER BAY

The Earle-Wightman House, built circa 1720, is located on Summit Street in the heart of Oyster Bay. Within walking distance to historic Raynham Hall, it too has a rich and interesting history as well as some resident ghosts.

On a blustery day in May, Joe and I headed over to the house to meet with Oyster Bay Historical Society director Denice Sheppard. On our arrival we were immediately taken back in time to three time periods, to be exact. Denice explained that the house is a reinterpretation of various time periods the house has seen. To our right was the oldest part of the house, which is set up as it would have been during the 1700s. To the left is a Victorian 1800s parlor, and off the 1700s wing is an addition that was more than likely added during the 1950s and is set up as such. Toward the back of the house is a small room that houses a gift shop and another room with a long table that at one time might have been a dining room. It was in this room that we conducted our interview.

There is a second floor that once contained three bedrooms, but it is not currently open to the public. Eventually, the Oyster Bay Historical Society would love to use the space for additional research materials. Its main headquarters is located directly behind the Earle-Wightman house at the Angela Koenig Center, which is a state-of-the-art repository containing a diverse collection of Oyster Bay's history. The space is also used for various lectures, exhibits and programs.

Earle-Wightman House.

The Earle-Wightman house is run by the Oyster Bay Historical Society but is owned by the Town of Oyster Bay. It was not always located on Summit Street. Its original location was on the westerly side of South Street, where the current firehouse stands. It was located there for nearly 250 years. The central part of the house was built in the traditional Dutch style, which is an indication that it might have been built by some of Oyster Bay's early Dutch settlers. The original foundation was made of tree trunks. The house has gone through many alterations throughout the years. It was moved to its current site in 1966, and oddly enough, the Summit Street address had been the location of an earlier firehouse.

The house is named after two prominent pastors who served the Baptist community in Oyster Bay for fifty-five years. They are the Reverend Marmaduke Earle and his grandson-in-law, Reverend Charles Wightman. Before their history is discussed, it is important to note that prior to their stay there, the house played an interesting role during the Revolutionary War.

Oyster Bay was occupied by the British from 1776 to 1783. The British decided to build their fort north of today's South Street in an area that is still known today as Fort Hill. The British built the fort there so they could protect Oyster Bay from "rebel" whaleboat riders who were crossing the Long Island Sound from Connecticut. At the base of this fort stood the house. In November 1778, more than four hundred members of the Loyalist Queen's Rangers came to Oyster Bay and strengthened the fort. Lieutenant Colonel John Graves Simcoe was in charge of devising a plan for the defense in case the village came under attack. At the time, only about 20 percent of Oyster Bay's population supported American independence. One of those people was a local politician and merchant known as Samuel Townsend. Samuel's son, Robert, was one of General George Washington's chief spies and worked under the name "Culper Jr."

Needing a headquarters and a place to stay during the winter, Lieutenant Colonel John Graves Simcoe established himself at the Townsend's home, which is now known as Raynham Hall. Other homes in the village housed junior officers and other enlisted men. One of the houses in which they lived was the Earle-Wightman House, where they remained for exactly six months. The British and Hessian garrison regiments also occupied the Earle-Wightman house at various times throughout the war.

In 1802, Reverend Marmaduke Earle left his congregation in Stamford, Connecticut, to accept a position in Oyster Bay, where he would be the head of a new academy that was being formed there. It was at this same time that he became the pastor of the Baptist Church, the oldest Baptist Church in Oyster Bay. In 1810, he left Oyster Bay for a short period of time. He had received an offer to be pastor at the Zoar Baptist Church in New York City. He accepted but resigned a few months later, returning to his posts at the academy and the church in Oyster Bay.

The congregation at the Baptist Church thrived under his direction and leadership, and he served there until his death in 1856 at the age of eighty-seven. He had been married to Mary Ferris, whom he had met during his time in Stamford, and they had eleven children together. Mary died in 1832 at the age of sixty-three. They are both buried in the Baptist cemetery on Orchard Street.

It is unclear who lived in the house between the British occupation and Marmaduke Earle, but it is clear that the reverend lived in the house during his entire time in Oyster Bay.

Twelve years after Reverend Marmaduke Earle died, Reverend Charles S. Wightman came to Oyster Bay in 1868. He served the Baptist congregation in Oyster Bay for more than a half century and was known by the locals as "Doc." He met and married Mary Earle, the granddaughter of Marmaduke. Mary had lived in her grandfather's house, and it became her married home. Charles and Mary did not have children, but Mary and her sister started a school for girls on Orchard Street. Mary died in 1901, and it is unknown how old she was at the time of her death. Charles outlived his wife by thirty-two years. He continued to live in the house after Mary's death and became very involved in the community and served on many committees while also serving as pastor of the church until his death in 1933. He was ninety-seven years old when he died. He and Mary are buried at the Wightman Family Cemetery in Connecticut.

As for the house, it is not known who lived in it from the time Reverend Wightman died in 1933 until 1954, when title records show Clausen W. Summers and his wife, Mary K. Summers, as owners. In 1961, it appears that Clausen Summers sold the house for $75,000 to Mr. Bruce Wood Hall of Muttontown, who was president of Hempstead Bank. At this time, the house was still located at 196 South Street, and the upstairs was rented out as an apartment. In 1966, Mr. Hall gave the house to the Town of Oyster Bay, and the town then moved it to its present location on Summit Street. In 1972, the Oyster Bay Historical Society turned it into a museum and used the space as its headquarters. It remains as one of the oldest houses in Oyster Bay.

It is no surprise that the Earle-Wightman house has a few ghosts. After touring the house with Denice Sheppard, we sat down and interviewed her about her experiences.

The oldest part of the Earle-Wightman House.

Denice, a lifelong resident of Oyster Bay, became director of the Oyster Bay Historical Society in November 2017 after the previous director retired. A lover of history, Denice has her own amazing story and family history, which she has written about in her book, *Footsteps of a Forgotten Soldier: The Life and Times of David Carll* (2016), which is the story of her great-great-grandfather. David Carll settled in Oyster Bay after fighting in the Civil War.

When she was a child, Denice would see spirits. She considers herself to be intuitive, something she might have gotten from her great-grandmother, who was Native American, and who used to read tea leaves in her parlor for the people of Oyster Bay.

"I can still see things on occasion," said Denice, "but I try not to. I live in an old home. Everybody in my family who lived in that house passed away, so there is a lot of activity. My husband didn't believe me at first, and then he realized. He started to hear things. It's really funny because people don't know how to embrace it or how to receive it."

When Denice first started coming to the Earle-Wightman house she felt very uncomfortable.

"Before I became director I used to come and speak to one of the past directors because I was really having a hard time coming into the house," she stated. "I didn't understand why. I would stand at the door and I would never come inside. The director would ask me why I wouldn't come in. I would just say, 'I'm uncomfortable' and wouldn't say why. When we became better friends, I eventually told him the reason. I heard, as I would come through the front door, a woman screaming. I didn't know who she was. I didn't know what she was. I just heard it—screaming." Denice paused a moment, remembering.

"I asked the director if he knew of anything. If there was anybody that he might have known who lived in the house," Denice continued. "He said he did know about a woman who had fallen out of the back window in the early 1900s. He said he believed she had killed herself. I said, 'Oh my goodness.' I never knew who it could have been, and I never asked after that."

During my research, there was nothing I could find that could validate the story, although it is quite possible it is true. The house would have been owned by Reverend Charles Wightman at the time. As we continued to talk about this, I suddenly smelled the distinct odor of cigar smoke. I asked Denice about this, and she told me that her grandfather had smoked cigars, so perhaps he was with us that day.

"I don't have a problem coming in here anymore, but I can probably hear more than anybody else," said Denice. "I don't hear the screaming that much anymore, but I'm usually not in here by myself. It's a beautiful house with a lot of character and a lot of energy. I have seen orbs, but I have not seen a physical face."

"Has anyone else mentioned feeling anything in the house?" I asked.

"I've had a couple of people tell me they have felt something totally different in the area by the gift shop—a change of energy. Nothing negative at all. But lights do go on and off here on occasion."

At that moment, all three of us heard a thump coming from upstairs, and we were the only ones in the house. We decided to get out the recorder and ghost box and see what we could pick up. The communication that day was extremely clear.

We started off the session by introducing ourselves, and Joe told the spirits that we were going to ask questions about the house, to which a spirit replied, "Good." I then told the spirits that Denice works here and that she loves the house. I asked them if they were happy that Denice was here. One spirit replied, "I don't know her." Another spirit replied, "I am here. That real camera?" My camera equipment was next to me on the table.

We then started asking questions about the woman who possibly died there. Here is the transcript:

> *Kerriann: Does the woman who killed herself in the house stay here?*
> *Spirit: Of course!*
> *Group: Of course!*
> *Denice: Oh, God!*
> *Joe: That's the woman…that's the woman we're sensing. You heard that right?*
> *Denice: Does she kill herself? Does somebody kill her?*
> *Spirit: It's possible.*
> *Spirit: Yes.*
> *Spirit: Killed her.*
> *Spirit: Insulting the mother.*
> *Denice: Hi, spirit. Did somebody kill her?*
> *Spirit: Yes.*
> *Group: Yes.*
> *Spirit: Who stabbed her?*
> *Joe: I'm feeling like it was a man…a jealous lover.*
> *Spirit: Yes.*
> *Spirit: No.*
> *Joe: So, he pushed her out of the window?*
> *Spirit: Yes.*

Joe: I heard yes.

Joe: She's okay now though, right?

Spirit: She's higher.

Joe: Higher…she's higher.

Spirit: Life without her…

Kerriann: Life without her…

Joe: Life without her—something.

Kerriann: So, did you want Denice to know this…that she's here?

Spirit: You could tell her…

Spirit: Awful. Awful. They found her a little later.

Spirit: In the grave.

Kerriann: In the grave, it sounded like.

Kerriann: Do you know what year she died?

Spirit: She died, age seventeen.

Spirit: Age seventeen, she was raised [to heaven].

Kerriann: Do you know what year she died?

Joe: What year did this woman die?

Spirit: Talk to her.

Spirit: Seventeen.

Joe: 1700s?

Spirit: Seventeen.

Spirit: He doesn't. [Joe doesn't understand the answer.]

Kerriann: What about the 1900s? You think it happened in the 1900s. Is that correct?

Spirit: I think Mister Smith do it.

Spirit: He's right.

Kerriann: Is there anything else you would like to tell us?

Spirit: No.

Spirit: They don't get it.

Spirit: The age. Tell him, he's right.

Spirit: No problem.

Spirit: Age approaching…

Group: 18!

Spirit: Correct!

Joe: All right, we got 18. Is that when the woman died? In the 1800s?

Kerriann: Or maybe it was the age.

Joe: Oh, the age 18?

Kerriann: Yeah, was she age 18?

Spirit: Yes.

Joe: That could have been a yes.
Kerriann: We just want to make sure you definitely crossed over. You don't
have to stay here.

Our conversation then shifted to the Revolutionary War and the Queen's Rangers:

Kerriann: Did Major Simcoe—
Spirit: Yes.
Kerriann: —come to this house?
Joe: I heard yes.
Spirit: He was.
Spirit: Oh, success.
Kerriann: So, Major Simcoe's men were housed here. The Queen's Rangers.
Spirit: Of course.
Kerriann: Of course.
Joe: Of course.

This next portion of the transcript was probably my favorite because the spirit said loud and clear "Sheppard," Denice's last name!

Joe: Hi spirits!
Spirit: Yep.
Joe: Yep.
Spirit: Okay.
Joe: Okay.
Spirit: No problem here.
Joe: No problem here. All right.
Spirit: Just perfect.
Joe: How you doing?
Spirit: Thank you.
Spirit: Got you.
Spirit: Rocking.
Joe: Okay, we're ready to ask some questions…
Spirit: Sheppard.
Group: Oh, Sheppard!
Joe: Thank you spirits!
Denise: You heard that?
Joe: You heard them say your last name, Sheppard.

Denice, who had never experienced working with a ghost box before, was completely in awe. We were all very happy that the spirits of the Earle-Wightman house were willing to communicate with us. Joe believed that Denice's energy and enthusiasm for the house was certainly a catalyst for the spiritual activity there.

I did not capture any orbs or apparitions on film when I took photographs that day, but Joe did some video recording on his phone and picked up some things. As he was exiting the room where we did the interview and walked into the front room, an orb flew from right to left. Another orb flew up the stairs as Joe made his way toward the older part of the house. In the recording, Joe also picked up two white noise EVPs. The first, a young female voice, says, "Hey," and then a low-pitched man's voice says, "Later on." I was still in the other room with Denice when Joe got these recordings.

Joe's analysis of the house is that the energy is good. The spiritual activity is calm but busy.

The Earle-Wightman house continues to be a wonderful part of Oyster Bay's history. We encourage you to visit and support the Oyster Bay Historical Society. While you're there, maybe you will pick up on a spirit or two as well.

7

LAKEVIEW CEMETERY

PATCHOGUE

Since the early 1800s, Lakeview Cemetery in Patchogue has been known to be haunted, and countless ghost stories abound. It is located on the corner of Waverly Avenue and Main Street next to the former site of a lace mill. A portion of the land had been donated by a generous and wealthy Patchogue resident, Ruth Newey Smith, in the late 1800s. The cemetery actually comprises five separate cemeteries: Episcopal, Waverly, Gerard, Rice and Lakeview, with Lakeview being the most recent. Over the years, the adjoining cemeteries have been referred to as Lakeview Cemetery.

The oldest graves, with some dating to 1794, can be found in the Episcopal, Gerard and Waverly portions of the cemetery. At one time, a Congregational Church had been located on the northeast corner of Main Street and Waverly Avenue and had been built in the late 1700s. Over 1,200 people are buried in the combined cemeteries, including at least thirteen Revolutionary War veterans, nine from the Civil War, twelve veterans from World War I and six from World War II. In addition, there are also three Vietnam veterans buried in the cemetery, as well as possible slaves in unmarked graves.

There are all sorts of strange stories surrounding the cemetery, and apparently, the earliest reported ghost sighting there appeared in the *Brooklyn Daily Eagle* in 1895. I have to admit that when Joe and I arrived there on an exceptionally windy fall day, I sensed immediately that this cemetery was an odd place. We met up with Patchogue Village historian and resident Hans Henke, who was a wealth of information. He even invited us back to his home, a mini historical society of sorts, where we poured over tons of research material, newspaper articles and personal notes from Henke, who spent years researching the cemetery. There was a time when the cemetery was badly neglected and extremely overgrown, and Henke was involved in the restoration project. He had a wonderful sense of humor and added some fun to the day, which was much needed once we learned about the disturbing fates of many of the people who lay in rest there.

A historical marker and stone appear to the left of the cemetery entrance and state that this was the location of Hart's Tavern, where President George Washington dined on April 22, 1790. The exact location of this tavern is unknown. However, there was another house supposedly located on the property from this same time period, and some believe perhaps the house and tavern are one in the same. A newspaper article from the 1800s makes mention of the "haunted house on Blood Hill," which was described as an "ancient house dating back to the Revolutionary War." There are various stories about where the name "Blood Hill" came from. Some say drunken sailors would visit Patchogue and get into fights and the streets were "running with blood." Other accounts state that because of the horrifying things that purportedly happened in the old house, it became known as the haunted house on Blood Hill.

Entrance to Lakeview Cemetery.

The original home was believed to have been owned by Squire Brewster Woodhull, a possible relative of Revolutionary War hero Nathaniel Woodhull. It is unknown exactly when the house was built, and by whom, but records indicate that Brewster Woodhull sold the house to Seba Smith and his wife, Elizabeth Oaks Smith, in 1860.

Seba Smith was the editor of a newspaper in Portland, Maine, as well as an author and political satirist. Elizabeth was an acclaimed author and poet. Edgar Allan Poe and Ralph Waldo Emerson were among her friends. Elizabeth was also a women's rights activist, and she and Seba were quite well-known in literary circles. They came to Patchogue in 1859 and purchased what was called the Woodhull Mansion a year later. The three-story, rambling house was located on the west side of the lace mill and next door to the older part of the cemetery. After they renovated the house, they called it the Willows, since it had been surrounded by willow trees. In 1868, only eight years after they moved in, Seba died. Elizabeth remained in the home for two years after her husband's death, moving out in 1870. Unfortunately, the house, during her husband's absence, had become quite rundown.

A number of families lived in the house after Elizabeth left. It is believed that its last occupants were a large group of Italian railroad workers who left the house abandoned and in disarray. Apparently, anyone who lived there did not stay long. Strange noises and other unexplained things occurred there, seemingly coming from the basement. It had long been rumored that prior to the abolition of slavery in New York in 1827, a "slave pen" was located in the basement of the house. Just who owned it at the time is unknown. Many Patchogue residents had claimed to hear screaming coming from the basement of the house and that some slaves were tortured and killed. It was rumored that some of the dead slaves were dragged out from the basement and buried in unmarked graves in the older portions of the cemetery. Even when the house was left abandoned, screams from the tortured souls could be heard, which led to the belief that the house on Blood Hill was haunted. There were numerous reports throughout the 1800s that the dark figure of a ghost carrying a blue flamed lantern could be seen walking in the old cemetery near the house. Residents of Patchogue would, at all costs, avoid walking near that part of the cemetery and would cross the street to the other side. The house burned down in a mysterious fire sometime between 1881 and 1893. Even when the house was gone, people claimed to have seen ghostly figures roaming the area where the house once stood.

Around 1895, more ghost stories and sightings had been reported after the burials of the victims from the *Louis V. Place* shipwreck. The land where the mansion once stood had been purchased by Augusta Smith Weeks, one of the four prominent Smith sisters of Patchogue. When she heard the story of what befell the sailors on that tragic day, she generously donated a plot and stones so they could have a proper Christian burial. Not long after the sailors were buried, ghostly activity increased, and many local townspeople reported seeing apparitions. It was rumored that a headless apparition, perhaps one of the doomed sailors, was seen more than once hovering over the graves of the newly dead. Others reported hearing screams and wailing sounds.

It was February 8, 1895, when the 163-foot, three-mast schooner *Louis V. Place* sailed from Baltimore for New York, carrying 1,100 tons of coal. It had left the port in Baltimore on January 28 and was off the coast of Cape Charles, Virginia, on February 5 when a terrible storm arrived. Temperatures were freezing, and the sails, hull and rigging were icing up. Two days later, severe winds and bitter cold made the crew's journey even more treacherous. The seas were getting rougher. By 7:00 a.m. on February 8, Captain William Squires had lost his bearings. The ship was leaking, and with everything being frozen, the vessel became completely unmanageable. The *Louis V. Place* was now in forty-eight feet of water, and Captain Squires decided to drop anchor. The lines were frozen, and the sailors, in their weakened state, could not free them. They were ordered by the captain to put on all the clothes they had and remain on the aft part of the ship. Ten minutes later, the ship hit a sandbar, and the pounding sea broke over the decks. The ship ran aground an eighth of a mile east of the Lone Hill Life-Saving Station on Fire Island. Two surfmen from the station saw the wreck and went for help. With the heavy surf, rescue crews could not launch their lifeboats. They made several attempts to launch a Lyle gun, a small cannon that shoots rescue lines. The sailors aboard the *Louis V. Pace* were so cold that they became debilitated and could not handle the lines. Trying to avoid the constant pounding of the icy waves, the men managed to climb into the ship's rigging and attached themselves to the masts.

The doomed sailors stayed like this for two days as the storm roared on. Captain Squires was the first to fall, his body being swept out to sea. Charles Morrison, the cook, was the next to fall. His body had been completely frozen. By 8:00 p.m., engineer Charles Allen, who had fought to stay alive, tumbled into the sea. Soon after, Gustave Jaiby, a two-hundred-pound man from Norway, and Fritz Oscar Ward froze to death and were found hanging from the lines. The only crew members left were Soren Nelson, Claus Stuvens and August Olson. Nelson and Stuvens found a way to make a shelter by cutting the lashing of the mizzen top sail, which had been furled. They were able to fit themselves into the hole. They made a desperate attempt to get Olson to join them, but Olson was trapped under the crosstrees and was unable to get around the mast. By Saturday morning, Olson had died. He was found frozen where he had been sitting.

Nelson and Stuvens kept themselves alive by hitting one another. More rescue lines were thrown to the two remaining men. Nelson was too stiff to move, but Stuvens managed to work his way down and grab the line. To his dismay, he dropped it because it became instantly heavy with ice. Having no other choice, he climbed back up to where Nelson was. Night came once again, and the weather grew colder. By midnight, the storm finally started to subside, and the men with the lifeboats were able to row out to them. Both Nelson and Stuvens were badly frozen.

The next day, a boat was launched, and rescuers went back to the shipwreck and cut down the bodies of the men who were frozen in the rigging. Eight plots with eight stones were set in Lakeview Cemetery, but only four of the sailors are buried there: Gustave Jaiby, Charles Allen, August Olson and Fritz Oscar Ward.

(Note: The names and spelling of the sailors' names in the historical research have varied. Gustave Jaiby's last name has also been listed as Gaiby, and the name on the tombstone reads Lars Gioby. August Olson has also been known as Gustaf Olson, and Fritz Oscar Ward as Mard.)

In a morbid detail, it is said that Gustave Jaiby was buried in his grave with a frozen piece of rope still stuck to his hand.

As for the fate of the two remaining survivors, Soren Nelson died of tetanus a few weeks later, on March 2, and Claus Stuvens went back to working on the sea. He had gained notoriety as the ship's sole survivor, and for many years, he gave lengthy interviews about the tragedy. Although he went back to the only profession he had ever known, he was never the same. He would often recall how he clung to the icy rigging for thirty-nine hours while he watched each of his shipmates freeze to death and be washed out to sea. He was eventually committed to Central Islip Psychiatric Hospital, and he died in 1902. One of the stones in the sailors plot at Lakeview Cemetery is his.

The only sailor without a stone was that of Charles Morrison, the cook. Some sources say his body was never found, while other accounts say because he was of "dark skin" he could not be buried on consecrated ground.

The stones for the sailors of the *Louis V. Place*.

There were rumors that he was buried in the dunes at a nearby beach in an unmarked grave. Apparently, when it was discovered that the man was in fact a Christian, some local townspeople went back to retrieve the body, only to find it missing. Many people believe it is Morrison who haunts the cemetery because he is not buried with his crew.

Another strange and interesting feature in Lakeview Cemetery is the twenty-two-foot-high memorial, which is located on the north end of the cemetery at the end of the center driveway. The monument was erected in 1909 by Ruth Newey Smith, sister of Augusta Smith Weeks. The Smith family were active community members, so Ruth took it upon herself to create a memorial in memory of the three sisters and their parents, who were among the first settlers of Patchogue. Four life-size statues representing faith, hope, charity and liberty sit atop the capstone, which measures five feet by four inches square. Wrapped around the monument is the genealogical history of the Smith family from 1641 to 1909 in three thousand words, consisting of eighteen thousand one-inch letters. The cost of the monument in 1909 was $5,000, and it is said to weigh approximately five tons. Elsewhere on the property is a large plot that contains the graves of the Smith family. Dominating this plot are four twenty-foot-high memorial columns. The site of these columns and monuments only adds to the oddity of this unusual cemetery.

Right: The twenty-two-foot-high Smith family memorial.

Below: The Smith family plot.

The last story regarding Lakeview Cemetery is probably the most gruesome of them all. It is the story of seven-year-old Helen Tiernan. On May 16, 1937, a sixteen-year-old girl named May Savage was walking through the woods near her house collecting flowers for her teacher when she made a grisly discovery. She came across the badly burned body of a young girl lying in the weeds. Her throat had been slashed. May ran and got a friend, and they returned with the police. As the police were searching the area for clues, one of the officers saw something moving in a tall patch of weeds. To his surprise, he found a young boy covered in bruises, also with his throat cut, but the cuts were not as deep as the girl's. The boy was rushed to the hospital, and the police continued the search, believing the mother of the children must be lying dead nearby. There was no body found. Instead, the search turned up a bloody knife, a bloody hatchet and a half-empty container of gasoline. An investigation began, and photos of the surviving five-year-old boy were in newspapers everywhere. The little boy was so traumatized that it was difficult to get information from him. All he remembered was seeing his mother hitting his sister. A nursery schoolteacher who recognized the boy from the papers came forward and identified him as Jimmy Tiernan, son of Helen Tiernan.

When the police approached her, Helen denied knowing anything about the death of her daughter and the attack on her son. After being questioned further, she finally confessed to the crimes. As the story goes, Helen, who was twenty-five, had been widowed for three years. She had recently met George Christy, a former boxer and restaurant worker, who became her lover. He moved into her small apartment, and Helen demanded the children call George "father." After a while, George got fed up with the children and the living arrangements and threatened to leave Helen. Panicked, she decided to leave the city and take a drive out to Long Island. She was familiar with the woods in Brookhaven Town from having attended a church retreat near there. She and the children boarded a train and headed out east to the location. She told the children she was taking them on a trip to the country. She entered the woods on the easterly side of Yaphank Avenue and walked approximately 150 yards into the woods, where the attacks took place. Meanwhile, George Christy was told by Helen that she had sent her children to live with her brother. The day after the atrocities, the two lovers spent time laughing and enjoying the beach and even had their photo taken.

It is unclear what happened to little Jimmy after he recovered in Patchogue Hospital. His only known relative was his grandfather, but he showed no interest in taking Jimmy in. Other sources say his uncle had considered it, but ultimately, it is believed that Jimmy might have wound up in an orphanage in New York City.

Helen Tiernan was convicted and sentenced to serve twenty years in the Bedford State Prison in New York. Expressing some remorse for murdering her daughter, she asked for money to be taken out of her account to be used for a burial.

The younger Helen Tiernan's body was taken to C.W. Ruland's Undertaking establishment in Patchogue, the same place where the sailors from the *Louis V. Place* had been displayed for the public. The building still stands today and is now Reece's 1900 restaurant. Helen was laid to rest in Lakeview Cemetery. It is said that only her grandfather had attended the funeral. Some workers from the adjacent lace mill took it upon themselves to purchase a headstone for Helen, which still remains today. For many years, flowers would appear at the gravesite, but no one ever knew who was placing them there.

Along with all the other ghostly activity reported at Lakeview Cemetery, there were numerous reports of people hearing the sound of a young girl crying, while others claimed to have seen the apparition of a young girl wandering among the tombstones.

Although Joe and I did get some ghost box communication, we did not connect with anyone specifically. Because of the wind, it was difficult for us to record any EVPs, and nothing else unusual happened during our time there. It wasn't until I started to write this story that something very strange happened.

As mentioned, I had received a lot of research material from Hans Henke, which I spent days going through. When I had everything in order, I sat at my computer and began writing the story. Working with Microsoft Word, I head each chapter title in all capital letters, indent centered, in Times New Roman, black, 12-point font. I am always hitting save so that I don't lose anything. On one particular day when I was about eight hundred words into the story, I saved the document, left it open and then left my home office and went downstairs. Nothing else remained open on my computer. The next day, I went up to my office ready to pick up where I had left off. To my utter astonishment, the chapter heading had been changed. It still read LAKEVIEW CEMETERY, but the indent was now to the left, the font was Calibri, the size of the font was 13.5 and the lettering was now a baby blue, not black. I sat at my desk and just stared at it for a few minutes. There was absolutely no one who had gone into my office the night before or the next morning. Perhaps one of the ghosts from Lakeview Cemetery wanted to make their presence known to me. There simply was no other explanation.

8

A PRIVATE HOME

HUNTINGTON

Throughout the years, there have been times when someone will contact me and ask me paranormal-related questions because he or she happens to be experiencing unexplainable things in their own home. I like to throw in a private home here and there in my books to show that regular, everyday people living in regular houses in non-historical areas can have spirits and ghosts among them.

I was contacted by "Lisa" (she wished to have her name changed for the sake of the story) in January 2019. She had emailed me and had gotten my name from Huntington town historian Robert Hughes, a friend of mine for many years. She had been trying to find out information about her house—if there was anything historical about the property or the house itself. She did a bit of research on her own and could not come up with anything. The reason for her inquiry was that she was trying to make sense of the strange things that were occurring in her home.

In her email, she had explained that she had been "experiencing paranormal activity" in the house for some time. So much so that she had actually contacted a group of paranormal investigators. On her own, she captured both video and audio footage, which she shared with me. She admitted that she was intrigued and curious and a bit apprehensive, and she was hoping I could give her some insight and put her mind at ease.

After reviewing what she sent me, I was intrigued myself. I gave Joe a call and forwarded him what she sent me with her permission. We both decided that if she was willing to share her story with us, it would be a great addition to the book. She agreed, and she invited us to come to her home to do an investigation.

For privacy reasons, I am not going to mention where in Huntington this house is, but I was granted permission to use the photo I took of it. At the time we interviewed Lisa, she had been living in the house for seventeen years. It had been her husband's home first. "Rob" had purchased it in 2002. When he bought the house, he liked the privacy of the property, and that is what really drew him to it. He had been told that the house was built in the 1930s. The house has the original doors and crystal glass doorknobs, along with some other beautiful old features. According to Lisa, he really loved the historical parts of the house.

When he bought the house, he found things in the garage that he didn't know anything about or where they came from. The items included an old whaling harpoon, old license plates from the 1950s and beautiful old fountains that Rob put out by the pool and front door. He found out from some neighbors who had lived in the area for a long time that his house was once a dairy barn that had been converted into a house. The second story was built to make it a legal two-story home. From what he was told, the people who built the house owned one hundred acres there. Lisa's research showed that town records from the mid-1950s did in fact show that the house

Outside "Lisa's" home.

had been a barn and part of a dairy farm and that it had been converted into a home. Unfortunately, further research I did on my end did not reveal any additional information.

The house sits in a quiet neighborhood on 0.75 acres. It is believed that three separate people had owned the house before Rob purchased it.

Lisa, at the time of this story, was thirty-six years old, and she lived in the house with her young daughter and a woman by the name of Kim, who lived upstairs in a legal attic apartment. Lisa's husband had died unexpectedly at the age of forty. They had been married for only eight years at the time of his death.

Kim knew Rob before she met Lisa because she used to dog sit for him. When Lisa and Rob got married, Kim soon became very good friends with them. Kim, whose husband died in 1999, agreed to join Joe, Lisa and me for the interview, especially since much of the phenomena occurring in the house has taken place in her area of the home.

"I always wondered [about ghosts]," said Lisa, "and I always thought, having the dogs, we would sense something or I would know. Then my daughter came along and I thought for sure when she starts talking I'd hear all sort of stuff. And then I kinda had given up on the idea, like, there must be nothing here. So, then Kim moves in, and I remember over the summertime, we were sitting outside, and Kim had asked me, 'So, have you guys ever heard anything?'"

"I was here maybe a year," began Kim. "I had borrowed a camera from my daughter because Mitzi [Kim's dog] was old, and I wanted to see what she was doing because I knew she would scream when I wasn't home. So, I wanted to see what was happening up there when I wasn't there." Kim is also a schoolteacher.

"So, I got the [video] camera for that reason," Kim continued. "I put it up in the living room so I could see what the dog was doing all day. I would look at the camera at night, and one day I was looking at it at work and I said, 'What the hell is that white thing in the living room?' I said to the teacher I work with, 'What's this?' and she said, 'Those are orbs.' And I said, 'No they're not.' She told me to go online and Google it. So, I Googled it, and I said, 'Oh my God, they're orbs, they're orbs, they're spirits!' So, I got really excited. So, now I'm checking that camera every night, and I'm getting stuff."

As the nights went on, Kim started seeing more and more orbs flying around the room when she wasn't home. She wondered if the spirits were all over the apartment, so she decided to move the camera into the bedroom.

At first, she hesitated because she wondered if she would be afraid of what she'd find. She had met a well-known psychic once who actually had told her that she had spirits in her apartment, and the psychic had never even been there. She did tell Kim that they were friendly.

"I decided to put it [the camera] in my bedroom, and it was like all hell broke loose! I was dumbfounded. I finally said something to Lisa about it. When I brought it up to Rob and showed him a few things, he thought that maybe it was dust."

"That was my first reaction too," said Lisa.

"Sometimes it would be weird. It would stop for a little, but then it would just flow. It would be at night, and it could be all night long. One, two, three orbs," said Kim.

"Maybe this is why the dog was upset. Maybe she was seeing them," I said.

"Now that you're saying that," Kim said, "I saw her follow something one night, and I saw her sitting up on my pillow, and the dog is blind. She can barely see me. It was so weird. I said to myself, well she can't see me, but she can see that because I see her watching it."

"Yeah," confirmed Lisa, "There is a video where you can see her looking."

"Sometimes it [the orbs] will slow down, and then it's just crazy!"

"And you were never afraid?" I asked.

"It didn't scare me," said Kim. "I said to myself I really don't believe they are harmful, because if they were, weird, bad things would have been happening. I never thought there was evil here. I have never felt scared."

"It was freaky at first, when she first started showing me the photos," Lisa added. "Kim kept telling me I should get cameras down here."

"Lisa, so after Kim spoke to you, did you start noticing things down here?" I asked.

"That was my biggest question," said Lisa. "I had never experienced anything before. I had no idea, and I really wanted to know was it [the spirits] here the whole time and I just never picked up on it, or did it start because Kim had moved in and the energy changed."

"But the psychic I knew also said it [the house] was like a portal. That they're just walking through," said Kim.

"Tell me about the animal face you saw in the orb," I asked, in reference to something Kim had told me earlier.

"It's a video of an orb, and when we stilled it, it looks like a Pomeranian," said Kim. "And in another one, I can't tell if it's a cat."

"So, after her videos started coming up, I always wondered whether it was the energy or if they were always here," said Lisa. "But then I got a photo of what looks like ectoplasm, and I had gotten a very clear orb that was really big in the kitchen. And then I go and get an orb downstairs in the basement."

"After your husband passed away, did you sense his spirit?" I asked Lisa.

"No, not really," she replied. "But then again, I would hear things and question myself, like, 'Are you sure it's not the house? Are you sure it's not this?'"

"Kim, what have you heard?" I asked.

"I would tell Lisa that it was hard for me to try and describe what it was. It would be like a knocking," Kim said. "There were times I would be woken up in the middle of the night. They would wake me up, and so whenever I started to go to bed, I'd say, 'No noises. I have to work in the morning. Be quiet.' But it was just weird. A lot of times, I would hear the knocking." She continued, "I said to Lisa a couple of weeks ago that I heard somebody say 'Kim!' and I thought it was Lisa, and I turned and answered, and nobody was there. Lisa was not at the door. There was nothing. But somebody called my name. You can hear some of the knocking in the videos. It's just odd. There are also strange noises of the door shutting. It doesn't scare me though."

As the four of us sat watching the videos, there was an interesting one of Kim in her bedroom while she was sleeping. The sheet mysteriously started billowing.

"I had shown the video to Lisa, and she brought it to my attention," said Kim. "I said, 'What? What are you talking about?' Then I looked at the video and thought, yeah, that's a little weird, but I said it was probably my foot. The way that it moved though—"

"It was like, billowing," I said.

"It was energy. That wasn't the sheet," added Joe.

"There was another video where you could see it moving up out of the covers and then you see an orb," said Kim.

"That could be an animal [spirit]," I said.

"It's possible," said Kim. "All my past animals used to sleep with me. Always. And there was one that used to sleep under the covers."

Our discussion then turned to EVPs. There were times when Kim had captured them on video. She played two for us.

"I talk in my sleep, and sometimes, they answer me back," said Kim. "One of the things they said was, 'I got you baby.' That's not something my husband would have said."

In another video, you can hear Kim say in her sleep, "Sixty-Five Broadway." Immediately following that you hear a voice say, "Huntington

Station." It is interesting to note that at one time Kim lived at 270 Broadway in Huntington Station. Number sixty-five no longer exists, and she never lived at that number, nor was there any significance. When Kim played us the video, we heard the EVP loud and clear.

It is interesting to note, when I had been playing back the recording of the interview we did that day, a mysterious static appeared on my recorder three times during the last eight minutes of the recording. That had never happened before, and there was no explanation for it.

Before our sit-down interview, Joe and I had done a walk around the house, including Kim's apartment. Joe had no previous knowledge of anything about the house or about the loss of either Lisa or Kim's husbands. I had arrived at the house first and told Lisa and Kim not to give any information to Joe.

As soon as Joe arrived, he immediately picked up on the spirit of a young man. As he stood listening, he turned to Lisa and announced that the male spirit was forty when he died—the exact age Lisa's husband was when he passed away.

"As soon as we walked into the first floor of the house," said Joe, "I sensed a man with a specific age of forty years old with dark hair. He told me that the room had been changed around since his death. The dining room and the living room had been switched, and he told me where he used to sit."

All of these things were confirmed by Lisa. We continued the tour of the house, and the number thirteen came to Joe as soon as he entered the daughter's room. At first, he assumed the daughter was thirteen, but then Lisa told him she was younger and that her husband's lucky number was thirteen. This was another validation. When we went back into the living room, my ghost meter started going off by a large chair. There was nothing electrical around it that could have set it off. Lisa confirmed that was the chair her husband always sat in. When we were done with the first floor, we made our way up to Kim's apartment.

"The energy changed as we walked up the stairs to the door," Joe said. "I felt lightheaded and out of breath. When we got into the kitchen, I told Kim she had lost a spouse as well and that he had died tragically. I then told her that he was someone who loved to cook and that he was a gourmet. I also saw a cruise that Kim and her husband went on. It was a big boat that left the United States. I said their cruise went to Bermuda and that her husband had a dry sense of humor."

Everything that Joe saw and felt was accurate and was confirmed by Kim.

"He said he does visit Kim at night," Joe continued, "and he smells like garlic."

This was validated by Kim, who said she smells her husband when he's around, and yes, it is always the smell of garlic. We then made our way into the bedroom, where Joe relayed the following: "I felt there was a lot of energy in the bedroom. Kim's husband stays upstairs, and another male spirit also visits Kim upstairs. While we were discussing this, I saw an apparition in Kim's bedroom moving around, sitting on the edge of the bed through the doorframe. I saw an apparition in the kitchen area as well, and I said that this particular person wore dark, square glasses. We agreed it wasn't Kim's husband but someone else."

Joe went around Kim's apartment and the rest of the house with a video camera, but he did not capture anything significant. I captured a faint orb in two of the several photographs I took in Kim's bedroom. The orb was located behind the bed on the wall above the headboard.

We did several ghost box sessions with Lisa and Kim, some of which were personal, so I did not include them here. Following is a small sampling of communication I can share with you:

Kim: Mom, are you here?
Spirit: Yes. She is sleeping. Older person.
Joe: Older person.
Spirit: Seventy. The mom.
Kim: Mom, are you around?
Spirit: The mom—right here.
Joe: I heard something about mom.
Kim: Yeah, I heard mom.
Joe: Mom, right?
Kim: Uh, Johnny, are you here?
Spirit: I'm here.
Joe: Johnny…was he a young person?
Spirit: Right.
Joe: Can he say the name of the people here?
Spirit: That's John/Johnny.
Joe: Who's sitting next to me?
Spirit: Bon voyage.

In this next excerpt I am asking the spirits what they think about being in the book and about the house being a dairy barn.

Kerriann: Are you happy we want to…this story in the book?

The bedroom where mysterious orbs fly around the room at night.

Spirit: Book?
Joe: Book?
Spirit: Don't worry. Thanks for coming.
Kerriann: Do you like using this tool?
Spirit: Yes.
Spirit: Me?
Kerriann: Is it easy for you to—
Spirit: I don't know!
Kerriann: —use this tool?
Joe: …The radio.
Kerriann: We would like to know more about the history. Was this a farm?
Spirit: Okay!
Kerriann: Was this a dairy farm?
Spirit: That's right.
All: That's right.
Kerriann: There were cows here?
Spirit: Was a farm.
Lisa: Do you like being here with all of us?
Spirit: Good.
Joe: Good.

Spirit: Hearing me?

Spirit: What's your problem?

Spirit: Keep the property. [We believe this was a reference for Lisa to keep the house and property—possibly a message from her husband.]

I had been in contact with Lisa weeks and months after our investigation there, and unexplained things have continued to happen in the house. Lisa sent me a few more videos of the orbs in Kim's room, and she wrote the following in an email to me: "Kim continues to have a flurry of activity, literally. It looks like it's snowing in this video! She has so many videos it's even difficult to keep up and go through them all."

Lisa admitted that she often forgets to turn her cameras on but that she does continues to hear a door closing on occasion when nobody is home.

Lisa ended her email with: "We all pretty much go about our daily routine without thinking about it too much at this point."

Lisa, Kim and the spirits have learned to coexist. As far as the activity in the house goes, Joe and I believe that both of their husbands visit and are watching over them and that perhaps there are some spirits that pop in from the dairy farm days as well. Because of their love for animals, we also believe that some of their past pets have come to them to bring them comfort. Overall, this private home in Huntington is a loving and positive place with lots of good energy coming from both those living and deceased.

9

HAWKINS-MOUNT HOMESTEAD

STONY BROOK

For those of you familiar with my books, you may recall past writings on the renowned Long Island genre painter William Sidney Mount. Along with his many talents, he was also a spiritualist. Although he has been dead for over 150 years, the communication we continue to have with him is truly remarkable. The ongoing relationship Joe and I have had with Mount has led us to delve a bit more deeply into understanding the man, the artist and the home in which he lived.

In the many years I wrote about William Sidney Mount, Joe and I were never able to get inside his house in Stony Brook, which I believed was an integral part of telling his story. I wanted to see where he lived, where he worked, where he painted. I had a feeling that if we had access to his house, his presence would be strongly felt.

As luck would have it, in December 2016, Joe and I were invited by Ward Melville Heritage Organization president Gloria Rocchio to visit the house and conduct an investigation. Needless to say, we were completely thrilled.

"We feel very strongly that this house is truly one of the jewels of this organization," said Gloria Rocchio. "The history is enormous, and it's on the National Register as well as the State Register, where it is listed as a very important site." She continued, "As for William Sidney Mount, I find his life fascinating."

On our arrival at the house, I knew immediately that Mount was with us, and within minutes of entering the house, phenomena began to occur.

Hawkins-Mount Homestead.

William Sidney Mount was born in Setauket on November 26, 1807. He was a musician and inventor and went on to become a well-known genre painter who meticulously captured the people and places around him on canvas. Much of his life was spent outdoors, a perfect setting for his paintings. Mount enjoyed fishing, walking, sailing and hunting. He believed in ghosts, and he believed in mediumship (communicating with those who have passed). In his lifetime, Mount had many of his own paranormal experiences. He often visited Hadaway house, located just down the road from where he lived, and he participated in séances there. Today, Hadaway house is the Country House restaurant and has its own resident ghost, which I have written about in the past.

William was the son of Thomas Shepard Mount and Julia Ann Hawkins and was one of five children. William's brother Henry encouraged him to paint as a child, and Henry used William as a helper in his painting shop. William later studied at the National Academy of Design in New York, and when he came back to Stony Brook, he began to paint scenes from everyday life.

According to the National Historic Landmark Statement of Significance, which designated Mount's farmhouse in 1965, "His genre scenes reflect his individualism, insistence on realistic portrayals, and his reliance on his own region and its people for subject matter."

William created several of his paintings in the attic of the house, which is also the space where he lived. He did prefer, however, to travel in a horse-drawn cart, which became his traveling studio and would allow him to paint on location. It was an interesting contraption that he invented and built himself.

Along with painting, William Sidney Mount did a lot of writing and kept countless journals. He would often write about his living situation and his discontent, which is what prompted him to find other locations where he could paint.

The earliest part of the house was built circa 1725 and was more than likely a one-room house with an entryway and chimney. Major Eleazer Hawkins, who was born in 1716, was the first documented owner of the dwelling. It is believed that during the 1750s he converted this small, preexisting structure to suit the needs of his growing family.

Eleazer and his wife, Ruth, had six children, one of them being Jonas Hawkins, who inherited the house from his father. Jonas and his wife, Ruth Mills, had nine children between 1776 and 1791 and enlarged the house further during this time period. In 1797, the house was also used as a tavern and was known as Major Hawkins Tavern. By 1800, it was listed as a tavern and store. It is interesting to note that Dr. Samuel Thompson (from the chapter on the Thompson House), according to his journals, purchased supplies at the store on a regular basis.

Along with being the proprietor of the homestead store and tavern, Jonas Hawkins was a farmer, as well as an active participant in the Revolutionary War. Although never confirmed, it has been speculated that Jonas could have played a role in the Culper Spy Ring. In addition, Hawkins's store was used as a Masonic Lodge where meetings were held.

Two of Jonas Hawkins's daughters married Mount brothers. Julia Ann married Thomas Shepard Mount, and Dorothy married Judge John S. Mount. Thomas and Julia Ann were married in 1801 and ran a farm and inn in Setauket. They had five children: four boys and one girl. As mentioned previously, one of their children was William Sidney Mount.

Thomas Shepard Mount died thirteen years after he married Julia Ann, when William was just seven years old. Needing help raising her children, Julia Ann moved back into the family homestead with Jonas and Ruth. When her father died in 1817, his estate was divided up among his children, and they could decide between themselves who would live in the house. It was stated that Ruth would remain in the home with whomever decided to live there. Julia Ann and her children, along with mother Ruth and Grandmother

Ruth Mills, lived in the house until their deaths. Julia Ann, having never remarried, died a widow in 1841. Each of Julia Ann's sons were given a fourth share of the family homestead on her death.

From 1817 to 1920, several generations of the Mount family lived in the Hawkins Mount house, which by this time was no longer used as a tavern or store. William and his brother Henry lived in New York City for some time, but William would often come back to Stony Brook to visit and work on his paintings. It wasn't until 1850 that he came back to the homestead to live permanently. William's area of the house was the attic, where he both lived and painted. To his dismay, he had to share the house with his brother Shepard and his family. William wrote of this discontent in his journal. "My paint room at this time is a garret on my own property. The first and second stories is occupied by my brother and his family. They invited me to place a sky light in the garret and now they say they have not room enough and now my ingenious sister-in-law, Mrs. S.A. Mount, says, she intends to place a bed for her children at the foot of the stairs leading to my studio. Undoubtedly to cramp my goings in and goings out."

In 1853, William wrote a letter to Shepard trying to resolve the situation. "I will thank you to move that trunk, chest, etc. from the passage that my right of way to my studio will not be obstructed. I wish you to regard this request in a kind spirit. Let us endeavor to live friendly. It was our mother's wish. Besides, it pays best at the end."

Shepard Mount died on September 18, 1868. William died just two months later at his brother Robert's house on November 19, 1868, at age sixty-one. Mary Bates Ford Mount, wife of brother Henry, continued to live in the Hawkins Mount house until her death in 1887. She had three children, all of whom were unmarried and remained in the house after their mother's death. They were the last members of the Mount family to occupy the house. It was daughter Evelina Mount who deeded the house and sixty acres to a relative, Charles Q. Archdeacon, in 1915. By 1919, the house had changed hands again and was purchased by Edward P. Buffet, who was extremely interested in the life and art of William Sidney Mount. Buffet made very little changes to the house. It was his goal to "preserve its integrity as a tangible relic of the artist's life."

Edward Buffet died in 1931, and by 1945, Edward's wife, Maude Miller Buffet, had sold the house and property for $10,000 to Ward Melville. Melville hired architect Richard Haviland Smythe to restore the Hawkins-Mount Homestead. The Victorian embellishments, which were added to the home by William Sidney Mount's relatives after he died, were removed, and the house was restored to its pre-Victorian period. Victorian windows were replaced with six-over-six sash, and the four dormer windows on the roof were also removed, among other things. Melville's vision was to create a museum where people could visit.

In 1952, he leased the house to the Museums at Stony Brook, then called Suffolk Museum. For a number of years, there were various families living in the house. A few of the past tenants believed that ghosts haunted the house, including that of Elizabeth Mount, William's first cousin. A young child who happened to be named Elizabeth reported that "a woman dressed entirely in white appeared at the foot of her bed." She was told the woman's name was Elizabeth. Other residents reported seeing people in Revolutionary War outfits.

The Ward Melville Heritage Organization (WMHO) owns the house today and leases it to what is now called the Long Museum of American Art, History and Carriages, which also owns a large collection of William Sidney Mount's work. The current tenant/caretakers who live in the house have stated that they have not experienced anything unusual there.

In keeping with Ward Melville's vision of restoring the house for the purpose of opening it to the public, the Ward Melville Heritage Organization has been continuing restoration of the house. Renovations began in 2016 and included putting on a new roof, stabilizing the floor and securing the foundation in the basement. Cosmetically, the house has been painted and repairs have been made to the core of the house, which is the early midsection on the first floor. WMHO hopes to open the house to the public on a small scale at some point. The last time it was open to the public was in the 1970s.

The house consists of two floors, plus the attic and a small basement. It sits on approximately two acres. Existing outbuildings include the original corn crib, carriage shed and a large barn.

The first time Joe and I visited the house was in April 2008. At that time, we were denied interior access to the house, but we still encountered phenomena outside. On a hot and windless day, a screen door on the side of the house mysteriously opened for us as if beckoning us to come in. It was in this same area where we recorded white noise EVPs with William Sidney Mount, which we have played for audiences at our lectures. From that point forward, Joe and I have each had experiences with William on a personal level. He has, in a way, become a spiritual guide for us, and he has been known to "pop in" on occasion. For me, it is usually when I am writing, especially if it is a story having to do with him. He is a wonderful communicator, and he himself experienced communication with those in spirit while he lived on the earth plane. Through his diaries we have learned that on a number of occasions he channeled the great artist Rembrandt, who served as a guide to William in regard to his paintings. It is no surprise that communication comes more easily with him.

When Joe and I arrived at the house in 2016, we met up with property manager Mike Colucci, who gave us access to the interior of the house. Mike had only one experience in the house, with a bathroom door on the first floor closing on its own. Oddly enough, not long after Mike left the premises, the door to the bathroom closed on its own for us as well. We made our way around the first floor, where construction and painting had been taking place. No one else was in the house at the time. At one point, Joe was in a nearby hallway while I stood in the main, older part of the house. I was holding my camera, but I did not start taking photos yet. I was standing still and simply looking around the room. All of a sudden, a large wooden board, which was leaning against a wall about four feet behind me, came crashing down to the floor. I jumped and then was speechless because there was absolutely no reason for the wooden board to have fallen. Joe quickly came in when he heard the noise, and we both determined that it was William Sidney Mount making it loud and clear that he was with us in the house.

As we continued our walk around, our cameras picked up some orbs on the second floor. We eventually made our way to the narrow staircase, which would lead us up to the attic. I cannot describe the feeling I had once we entered it. It was like going back in time, and William's presence was quite strong here. Joe had taken a photo of me looking up at the ceiling. The image revealed an orb in the area I had been looking at. Joe had also recorded orbs in movement when taking a video on his cell phone.

In a photo I took of Joe in the attic, small orbs could be seen on his back, as well as on the wall. One of the most fascinating things we discovered was a shelf located next to a window toward the back end of the house. Painted on a wooden bracket that supported the shelf was a colorful palette with names of the colors written beneath them. We were told by Gloria Rocchio that this more than likely was William's palette and his handwriting. It was a remarkable discovery. I took several photos in this area, and in one of them, an orb appeared not far from the shelf. Could the orb have been William Sidney Mount?

The attic was alive with energy, so we decided we would use the recorders in this area. Since we had already gotten white noise EVPs outside during

Large orb in the room where the wood mysteriously fell.

Joe in the attic with orbs on his back and around him.

our past investigation, Joe thought it best to use the ghost box this time around. The ghost box would generate clear-voice, real-time answers to our questions. Joe recorded our session on both his Droid phone's memo recorder and his handheld Olympus digital recorders.

As Joe has said, "The recording with Mr. Mount became one of our longest and most comprehensive dialogues with spirits. It was a great example of intelligent two-way communication. Often, the dialogue was humorous and loving, another indication of the intelligent communication."

Here is an excerpt from our dialogue with William Sidney Mount, which took place in the attic:

Joe: We're going to do the ghost box recording session.
Spirit: Exactly!
Joe: Okay Mr. Mount, welcome.
Joe: Mr. Mount, are you here?
Spirit: A couple of days before.
Joe: Kerriann is here; Kerriann say your name.
Joe: We'll introduce ourselves to the spirits.
Spirit: Love you!
Kerriann: William, it's me. I know you want Joe to call you Mr. Mount.
Spirit: Exactly.
Kerriann: But I can call you William? Yes?
Spirit: Yes.
Kerriann: OK.
Joe: Uh, hi spirits. How are you?
Spirit: Fifth dimension.
Joe: It's a radio. That's right.
Spirit: It's scanning.
Joe: On FM—that's correct.
Kerriann: William, are you happy that we're in your house?
Spirit: Investigational.
Kerriann: William, the room that we're in now.…Is this where you painted?
Spirit: Yes.
Kerriann: Was your brother Sheppard in this room?
Spirit: Unfortunately.
Joe: Yeah, thank you for letting us come in here today.
Spirit: All right.
Joe: My sister has a painting done by your brother.

Shelf in William Sidney Mount's studio showing palette paint samples.

Spirit: Yes, I know.

Joe: We're having fun.

Spirit: Some fun.

Joe: Thank you.

Spirit: Good.

Spirit: Thank you.

Joe: You're welcome.

Spirit: Look at this sh—t!

Joe: You know, we were at the Ketcham Inn in Center Moriches. When we first went there it was just a bunch of boards torn up and now it's so beautiful in there. You ever been there? Could you take your soul there and take a look and see how pretty it is?

Spirit: Love it!

Spirit: Jamming!

Joe: Let me know when you're back.

Spirit: Hello, Joe.

Spirit: We're here.

Joe: Hi! You're right here. OK. Yeah, the Ketcham is very pretty.

Joe: I think your house will be really pretty when it's done.

Joe: Ah, we're going walk downstairs and keep the ghost box on.

Spirit: Got ya!

Joe: Thank you.

Spirit: I saged this room.

Joe: This is fun. We had a lot of fun!

Spirit: Yeah.

Spirit: We love that, Joe.

Spirit: Sweetest person.

Joe: I know you're making sentences. Make one more sentence and I'm going to go downstairs.

Spirit: We're set.

Joe: We're set? OK.

Spirit: Why?

Joe: Why what?

Spirit: You did a flash to me?

Joe: Oh, why did we do the flash?

Spirit: Mhmm.

Joe: We don't use powder for a flash anymore.

Joe: Hello.

Spirit: Spirit?

Joe: Spirits, yeah.

Spirit: Hi!

Joe: Yeah, what's up? We're going downstairs now.

Spirit: I know.

Joe: Oh, it's a great place!

Spirit: Protect this space!

The home in which Mount lived and painted remains a great example of American vernacular architecture, with a wonderful and rich history.

William Sidney Mount has continued to find ways to communicate with us and make his presence known, even as I sat to write this story. If you would like to know more about this fascinating man and his views on religion, spiritualism and mediumship, you can read his complete story in my book *Historic Haunts of Long Island*.

10

Locust Valley Library

Locust Valley

A library having ghosts? Who would have thought, but when Joe and I headed over to check things out at the Locust Valley Library, we discovered that many people had experiences with the resident ghosts. As we delved deeper into the history of the library, we were not surprised, because the building was a mecca of community activity since the early 1900s.

We made our visit to the library a few weeks before Christmas 2019. Joe and I met with Kathy Smith, director of the library, and Amy Dzija Driscoll, the director of the North Shore Historical Museum. They told us about the library's rich and diverse history.

The original library was located on Bayville Road, where it occupied the first floor of the Bailey house, also known as Thurston Cottage, which was built in 1865. The library was established in 1909 under the direction and leadership of the famed publisher Frank Nelson Doubleday, who was very influential in the development of Locust Valley, along with Frederick A. Horsey, Edward Latting, James T. Mitchell Jr., Dr. Richard F. Seaman, Charles F. Williams and Edward M. Ward. A $300 donation was given to the founders from the newly formed Matinecock Neighborhood Association. The first president of the library was Doubleday's wife, Heltje DeGraff. A charter was granted to the library from the New York State Regents in September 1910, and by 1914, the library was growing, and a new location was needed. The Matinecock Neighborhood Association built a community center on Buckram Road called the Matinecock Neighborhood House, and it generously supplied space for the library. The house itself was built through monetary donations from the local residents, carpenters, masons

Locust Valley Library.

and plumbers, among others, who provided their services free of charge. The large, estate-like structure with a large front porch was built on the crest of a hill on approximately three wooded acres.

In 1730, Locust Valley was actually known as the village of Buckram, where early settlers farmed the land and harvested fish and shellfish in the surrounding waters. There were many creeks and brooks that made their way through the village and became a great source for the settlers. By damming the creeks, they created water flow to run several small mills, including a gristmill, sawmill, paper mill and cider mill. Another mill, called a fulling mill, produced buckram, a type of course fabric, thus where the village name Buckram came from. In 1856, the name was changed to Locust Valley, since there was an abundance of locust trees, and the town was situated in a valley. In 1900, residents tried to change the name again to Matinecock, after the Matinecock tribe that once lived there, but they were unsuccessful. Buckram Road was actually a footpath for the Matinecock Indians as they made their way along the banks of the Chagechageon Brook. Buckram became an official road in 1703, and several homes were built there.

By 1869, the railroad arrived and still runs through the woods behind the present-day library on Buckram Road. At the end of the nineteenth century, large tracts of land were purchased by wealthy families coming from the city who wanted to build summer homes near the water.

"The Matinecock Neighborhood Association was a civic association formed in 1908," said Amy Driscoll "It was mainly bankrolled by the wealthy Gold Coast estate owners, but all the community were members. They paved roads, they damned up Beaver Lane. They did civic-type things. This building was built because they realized they needed a community center. Locust Valley is an unincorporated hamlet. There wasn't a Town Hall. It's still like this. So, they built this building in 1914, and they called it the Matinecock Neighborhood House."

Over four hundred people attended the opening in September 1914. There was a large auditorium on the upper level where dances were held, as well as plays, movies, card parties, recitals and other social gatherings. In the basement was a two-lane bowling alley, a pool table and a social room. Outside were tennis courts, which can still be seen today. The basement eventually housed the Locust Valley Hook & Ladder Company. By 1915, the library was operating two substations, one in the public school and the other in the Neighborhood House.

As the years went on, other organizations, such as the Boy Scouts, Girl Scouts, the choral society, a drama club, the Home Defense Corps and the Red Cross, began to have their meetings at the Neighborhood House. The association also offered cooking classes and English language and wellness classes, and in 1918, the house even served as an infirmary during the flu epidemic.

The community center was open every day, including Sundays, with seven hundred to one thousand people in attendance weekly. The numbers grew as the years went on. The Neighborhood House remained financially supported by the community.

"The way the Neighborhood Association operated, basically, was that they funded the house, they funded the activities and the members of the community contributed if they could," said Amy Driscoll.

In 1919, a captured German cannon was presented by the French government to Henry P. Davison, who was the chairman of the American Red Cross War Council. He, in turn, donated it to the residents of Locust Valley, where it was "to be preserved as a memorial of their patriotic sacrifices, services, and contributions during the World War 1917–1919." It still proudly sits outside the library today, along with an honor roll listing the 132 men in the area who served in the armed forces.

By 1923, the space that housed the library became limited. Frank Doubleday decided to provide the funds for the construction of a new library wing. Then, around 1930, with the onset of the Great Depression, the community could no longer sustain the Neighborhood House, and activities there began to dwindle. By 1936, the building was boarded up for twelve months, but the library wing stayed open. Prior to that, in 1934, Mr. Doubleday bequeathed $2,500 to the Locust Valley Library Association, which formed the base for the present-day endowment fund. By 1937, the library trustees took an interest in taking over the deed and full control of the Matinecock House. After a heated meeting and close election, the Locust Valley School District made the decision to take on the building and grounds for the purpose of creating a public library, which would cost taxpayers an additional $3,000 a year. Subsidies came from the rental of the building for certain events, along with the rental of the bowling alley and tennis courts.

The library was renovated in the early 1980s and again in the late 1990s as the needs of the library and the collections grew. Today, there are three floors, two of which are open to the public. The third floor served as a caretaker's apartment for a number of years and now serves as office space. It is also home to the Locust Valley Historical Society, which was formed in 1983. All these years later, the library still serves as a community center for the residents of Locust Valley. The basement is now a community center where patrons still gather for lectures, entertainment and other events.

There has been talk of the library having ghosts for years, and when Joe and I did our walk around with Amy, Joe sensed a lot of energy coming from all of the people who came through there.

"I felt a general calmness and happy energy all around," said Joe. "The energy changed dramatically when going from the new wing into the main building and also upstairs where the old stairways are with the wooden steps made of pine. Several times, both Amy and I felt cold spots that moved toward us."

We asked Amy and Kathy Smith if either of them have had experiences.

"I always wanted to see the ghost," said Amy, "but it hasn't happened. I love this building. I love history. I'm like, come on, what about me?" she laughed.

Kathy hadn't had any experiences either, but she did admit that she doesn't go looking for it.

"I have heard the stories, though," said Kathy. "Some of the staff have said they've experienced things. One person was tapped on the shoulder when no one was there, and some people have seen faces. There is a door downstairs. Sometimes I'm the last one out on a Friday night and all the lights are out, and I have to walk down the stairs. The door at the bottom of the stairs has a self-closing mechanism that sounds like it's moaning as you leave. And every time I hear it, I'm like, 'I'm getting out of here!'"

"Mind over matter," I said.

"Yes," Kathy answered. "The power of suggestion."

"That's what you have to figure out," said Joe. "What is real and what is just our imagination. For us, it sometimes makes it difficult to actually verify anything specific [during an investigation]. It's kind of like a smorgasbord of paranormal events."

We did have the opportunity to speak with a few employees who had some amazing stories to share with us.

Kathy Jones is head of circulation at the library and has worked there for twenty-one years.

"I had never heard of anything going on here before I came," Kathy began. "I had been doing programming before I was doing this job, so I was always busy running around here or there. One day I was upstairs [on the third floor], and out of the corner of my eye I see someone dressed in white, and she's twirling, like dancing. And I'm like, 'Did I see that?' And then, of course, it's over. I did see that a second time in the community room. The same thing, out of the corner of my eye. I see a woman in this beautiful white dress, and she's having a great time," Kathy laughed. "And she's twirling! It seemed to be the same spirit in two different places."

"How long did it last?" I asked.

"Oh, that was just, like, seconds."

"How old was she?" asked Joe.

"Forty-ish, blondish hair…sparkly."

Kathy had these experiences approximately ten years apart. And she hasn't seen anything since. She did say there were a few other people at the library who have had experiences, people she believed are sensitive to these things.

"We had a custodian who worked here," continued Kathy, "who came running out of the room on the third floor and said, 'Did you tap me on the shoulder?' I said to him, 'No.' He said that he was sitting at the desk and something tapped him. He turned, and nobody was there. And he's not the kind of person to make things up. There was one evening when I was working with Doris and David, this was a long time ago now, and as we're walking out the back door, the lights were all shut off, and out of the corner of my eye, I look up [at the mezzanine level], and I thought I saw a face in the reference area. And I'm thinking, we don't want to leave somebody behind here. So, I'm thinking someone's still up there. I said to David, 'Did

Third-floor hallway, where paranormal events have occurred.

you check upstairs?' and he said, 'Yeah, no one's up there,' then he bolted and ran out," Kathy laughed. "And I'm standing there in the dark and we're like, 'He left us!'"

"I think this was a really active place with a lot of energy," I said.

"Agreed," said Joe.

"And they're either passing through or their energy is left behind," I said.

"It could be imprints of people who were here," said Joe.

Lauren Wallach, children's librarian and youth services, told us the following, "When I first started working here, I sensed that there were spirits here," said Lauren. "I spoke with Kathy Jones, and she confirmed it. I've never seen anything, but walking down that hallway on the third floor, it gives me a strange feeling. You feel this buzz happening. I look around as if I'm going to see someone, and there's no one there."

I spoke with a man over the phone, whose name is Tom, about his experience. He is a current employee and custodian at the library.

"I'm the first one there in the morning, so I go downstairs and turn the lights on, and everything is fine. I go upstairs [and do the same], and then I come back down, and a whole shelf of books is on the floor in the children's area. It happened about a year or so ago," said Tom. "Then, you know how

The children's library, where books have mysteriously come off the shelves.

the exhaust fans are on in the bathroom? They usually go on when somebody walks into the bathroom. Well, the fan would go on by itself, when no one went in there. I only had those two experiences, but I try and keep it to myself so no one thinks I'm crazy," Tom laughed. "I try to stay away from it."

In another phone interview, I spoke with Doris DeQuinzio, a retired library clerk who worked at the Locust Valley Library for sixteen years.

"It's a great library to work for, and it's historical," Doris began:

> *I used to work anywhere from the children's area, which is on the lower level, to the third floor, which is where the offices are. When I was working in the children's area, I was at the circulation desk, and it was around six o'clock in the evening, and I saw, like, a white flash go by. I saw that again on the third floor. I never saw it on the main floor. When I saw it on the third floor, I saw it when I was in the kitchen. It passed by the kitchen door. The third time I saw it was again on the third floor. This time I was sitting at my desk in the office. I turned around, and actually, this time, I saw a figure, and it was a male figure. It just walked past the door. It wasn't a figure that was human, that you could touch. It was the combination of a spiritual figure and a human figure, and it was definitely male.*

Doris continued, "At the time, one of our custodians had passed away, and he worked here for years. I could have sworn it was him. He wasn't dressed as a businessman, and he wasn't dressed casually. He was dressed in some sort of work-type clothes. The face was not clear."

"It is so rare to be able to catch something like that," I said. "You have to be in the right place at the right moment. If it was the custodian, it could have been his residual energy that caused the phenomenon."

"I remember saying to my co-worker, 'I just saw Doug pass by.' Even though I lived in Locust Valley for years, I never heard anything about it [ghosts being here]. It really is just a charming old library."

Joe and I did have a short ghost box session with Amy on the day we did our interviews and investigation, but we found that most of the answers we received were fuzzy and inaudible. We conducted the session on the third floor, and the reception overall might not have been good. I asked if there was a woman who likes to dance here, and we received a loud "No." When Joe asked if there were any Native Americans here (from before the Neighborhood House was built), the spirit said "Eleven" and then the spirit said, "This is still our country."

Although we did not receive an extensive ghost box recording, and our photographs revealed nothing unusual, it doesn't mean that the spirits of the Locust Valley Library do not exist. Between the expansive history, the number of people who walked through the library's doors and the incredible accounts from staff members, Joe and I agreed that the Locust Valley Library is definitely on the list of one of Long Island's haunted historic places.

11

LONG ISLAND MARITIME MUSEUM

SAYVILLE

When Joe and I first arrived at the Long Island Maritime Museum in Sayville, I was absolutely amazed by how big the museum was and all of the outbuildings and property surrounding it. It was like its own little village. I couldn't help but wonder why it had never occurred to me to go there prior to our investigation. All I can say is that I've been missing out. Sitting on approximately fourteen bucolic acres that overlook the Great South Bay, the museum houses a treasure-trove of Long Island's maritime history.

Little did we know that ghostly activity abounds, and that the spirits were waiting for our arrival so they could show us a thing or two. We met up with Terry Lister-Blitman, the museum's executive director, who had many unexplained things to tell us. We had much to see that day, but our first stop, and the place of our interview, was in the library.

"So, this room is the library," said Terry as we made our way into the beautiful room lined with books and sailing trophies. "It's not original to the building. The building was originally built as a garage."

Terry continued:

> The estate belonged to Florence Bourne, and she was the daughter, one of a number of children, of Frederick Bourne. In Oakdale, Frederick Bourne built an estate. His main home was in Manhattan. His summer home was the estate in Oakdale. When Florence got married, he gifted her five hundred acres of his estate, and that's where we're sitting now. He also built her a

home as a wedding gift. That's the house you see by the golf course [West Sayville Country Club]. *That was her main home. Now it is occupied by Suffolk County Parks as well as Lessings Hospitality Group.*

So, this [building] *was her garage. She would drive her vehicles in, and she had a chauffeur who lived in this building on the second floor who maintained her car collection. This room* [presently called the Elward Smith III Library] *was added on later.*

We sat with Terry and learned more about the Bourne family. Frederick Gilbert Bourne was born on December 20, 1851. He was the son of a Boston minister. The family eventually moved from Boston to New York City. The family had some money but not enough to send Frederick to college, so he found work at the Mercantile Library as a clerk. There he met millionaire Alfred Clark, who was the president of the Singer Sewing Machine Company. Coincidentally, Frederick sang in the church choir in Mr. Clark's church. Mr. Clark admired Frederick's singing voice, and he often invited him to come and sing at his home when he hosted parties and gatherings. As Mr. Clark got to know Frederick, he admired his work ethic and personality, and he eventually offered Frederick a small job in his company. Over the course of just a few years, Frederick made his way up the corporate ladder and into a management position.

Long Island Maritime Museum.

Twenty years after accepting that first offer, Frederick was the secretary of Singer's board of directors. By 1889, when the firm's president, George McKenzie, was retiring, Alfred Clark endorsed Frederick. At age thirty-eight, Frederick Bourne became Singer's fifth president, a position he would hold until 1909. The company flourished under his guidance. He expanded global production and international sales, and he had a strong commitment to advertising the product. It was under his leadership that the first electric Singer sewing machine was created.

On February 9, 1875, Frederick Bourne married Emma Sparks Keeler of New York, and they went on to have nine children. Their first child, Arthur, was born in 1877. The Bournes' primary residence was in New York City, and wealthy New Yorkers during the late nineteenth century often built their summer residences on the shores of Long Island. Oakdale became a prime location for elaborate estates because of its proximity to the Great South Bay and the two-thousand-acre South Side Sportsmen's Club. After the Bournes summered in Oakdale for a number of years, Frederick finally purchased four hundred acres known as Oakdale Farm from Colonel William H. Ludlow for $80,000. The property was located on the Great South Bay, south of Montauk Highway. It was during the peak of the oyster industry, and the Long Island Railroad had just made its way out to Sayville. Bourne's beaux arts–style estate was designed by Ernest M. Flagg and was patterned on the White House. Built of brick with white marble trimmings, the house was 300 feet long by 125 feet wide and had approximately one hundred rooms, plus a portico, esplanade and courtyard. Work began in 1897, and local men from the community were hired to build the house and magnificent grounds. Frederick called his home Indian Neck Hall. It was completed in 1900, just in time for Frederick and Emma to celebrate their twenty-fifth wedding anniversary with an elaborate party.

Throughout the years, Frederick Bourne continued to purchase additional property, increasing the size of his estate. On his death in 1919, his landholdings consisted of nearly two thousand acres. During his lifetime, his plan was to provide his children with property and residences of their own.

When daughter Florence married Anson Wales Hard in 1908, Bourne gave his daughter and son-in-law five hundred acres located on the southeast corner of his estate, which stretched from Montauk Highway to the Great South Bay.

In 1909, renowned Sayville architect Isaac Green was called in to design the young couple's estate, and construction soon began. The Hards called their two-story, fourteen-room colonial revival home Meadow Edge, after the sprawling salt meadows that buffered the Great South Bay near their home. The large garage was built later in 1920 and replaced a smaller garage that was constructed at the same time as Meadow Edge. The new garage housed an assortment of cars as well as a machine shop. The living quarters for the chauffeur and his family were located upstairs. In 1928, the addition to the garage was built to display Anson Hard's trophy collection. He was an avid sailor, sportsman and competitor.

The Hards lived at Meadow Edge until Florence and Anson's divorce in 1932. Around 1939, when the Second World War began, Florence and the children moved out of the main house and into the garage, where they occupied the second floor of the eastern portion of the building. By the mid-1950s, she had left the Meadow Edge estate and moved to Stamford, Connecticut. In 1966, Florence Bourne Hard, now Florence Bourne Thayer, sold the property to Suffolk County for $1,250,000, with the stipulation that the property not be developed for private commercial use. It was the last of the original Indian Neck estate to remain in the hands of the Bourne family.

Today, the estate is home to the West Sayville Country Club at the Charles R. Dominy County Parks and the Long Island Maritime Museum. Elsewhere on the property are Florence's greenhouses, which now house G.R.O.W. (Greenhouse Recreation Opportunities Workshop), which is sponsored by the Developmental Disabilities Institute.

As for the Frederick Bourne mansion, it is currently a magnificent catering venue specializing in weddings and is run by the Lessings Hospitality Group.

Shortly after Suffolk County acquired the estate, a group of concerned citizens founded the Suffolk Marine Museum on December 16, 1966. Its purpose was to collect and preserve artifacts of Long Island's maritime history. The museum opened its doors to the public on May 1, 1968, and it received its absolute charter from the New York Board of Regents in November 1983. The newly formed board of trustees worked with the Suffolk County Department of Parks, Recreation and Historic Preservation to help raise funds to obtain a variety of maritime collections, including watercraft vessels, historic buildings, machinery, artifacts, ship models, maps, charts and books and maritime crafts and trades.

By 1993, Suffolk County ceased support, and the operations were privatized under the corporate identity of the Long Island Maritime Museum. It has been running programs, exhibits and events since.

What makes the Long Island Maritime Museum unique is that it is more than just a museum. All of the buildings on the museum's grounds are "living pieces of history, each offering a glimpse of different aspects of 19th century life."

The main building (the garage) offers exhibits that explore the U.S. Life-Saving Service, shipwrecks, local history, model ships and more, along with the library, which has books, nautical maps and charts. The main building also houses offices and a gift shop.

Elsewhere on the property is the Bayman's Cottage, circa 1890; the Frank F. Penney Boat Shop, where you can actually see boats being built; the Everitt-Lawrence Small Craft Building; and the Oyster House, which is used as an educational exhibit about shell fishing on Long Island. All of the buildings are open to the public. In addition, the historic oyster sloop *Pricilla*, circa 1888, is located on the waterfront and, in season, goes out on two-hour sails on the Great South Bay. *Pricilla* was a working oyster sloop that went through a major renovation right on the grounds of the Long Island Maritime Museum. This U.S. Coast Guard–certified vessel, can take up to thirteen passengers.

Before we toured the property and these wonderful outbuildings, we continued our interview with Terry in the library of the main building and then started talking about ghosts. While we were sitting there I couldn't help but notice that the sailing trophies were shelved around the room until it got to the left of the fireplace. There was a shelf with an empty space. It was such a well-put-together room, so I thought it was odd that no trophies appeared in this one area. I asked Terry about this.

"In this room, we house the majority of our trophy collection," Terry began. "All of the trophies on this side of the room are considered active trophies. So they are still issued to individuals after a race is complete. They are taken care of and monitored by the Great South Bay Yacht Racing Association. The trophies that are on this side of the room, and in the case, are all retired. The spot that is empty, to the left of the fireplace, is where the trophies fly off the shelf." Terry paused and looked at us for a moment. She had definitely piqued our interest.

"Originally, the trophies went from the fireplace all the way over. The first time I witnessed a trophy coming off the shelf was five years ago, maybe. I was standing here, and one of our employees was standing here." Terry got up from her chair and went over to show us exactly where they had been standing. "The director at the time, Steve Jones, was standing here, and his back was to the shelf. One of the trophies from that area just flew off the shelf and hit the floor right here," she pointed. "So, we all were like, OK, and we were making jokes about it. We thought it was odd, and that was it.

The trophy was damaged. The base of the trophy was dented so it couldn't stand up anymore, and our collections manager, Arlene, took it and did her best to bend it back out. She then returned it to its shelf," Terry paused.

"Don't tell me it came off again," said Joe.

"Yes," Terry said.

> Then there was this one instance, I don't remember how long after, where I came in the morning and the trophy was on the floor again in the same spot. And I just thought, OK, this is ridiculous. I gave the trophy to Arlene and said to her, "Don't put it back. It's ruined." She says OK, and she takes another trophy that she had up in the attic, and she put that one on the shelf. I came in the next morning, and the trophy, the second one that was placed there, was on the floor. And that one was damaged. I said to Arlene, "You know what? Don't put it back because someone is going to get hit, and there's going to be a problem, and we're ruining the trophies." Then the trophy next to it also came off the shelf, so from that point on, I said, "Don't put anything back in that spot," and it's been empty ever since.

"That is unbelievable," I said.

"Then there was a day when Arlene and I were standing right here, and we were working on the photos that are included in the exhibit in the rear gallery. There was foam core, we're gluing, we're cutting, we're doing all this stuff, and the doors to the library are always open, and we had a visitor who started to walk into the room, but he stopped about right here," Terry demonstrated. "I guess he was wondering if he should come in because he didn't want to disturb us. All of a sudden, this panel [on a glass display case] exploded."

"Really?" I said.

"It [the glass] just exploded and then the frame fell onto the floor. The man felt bad and started saying, 'I didn't touch anything,' and we're telling him it's OK. We had to calm him down. We cleaned it up and then we had to get the glass replaced."

Terry then went on to tell us about the other unexplainable things that she had experienced.

"I have the tendency to work late sometimes in the wintertime," Terry said. "I would be by myself, and there were many instances where I would hear from my office furniture being moved—like case pieces, dressers, large wood pieces of furniture being dragged." (Terry's office is a small cutout room off the library.)

The library where trophies have flown off the shelf. Note the empty space on the shelf to the left of the fireplace.

The glass display case that shattered for no apparent reason.

"It was coming from the attic, and I know there are no pieces of furniture in the attic. It would happen again and again. I wasn't afraid. I was annoyed. I remember saying, 'OK, this is what we're doing now?' Then it stopped for a while and then there was a knocking at the door," Terry pointed to a door that led to the back. "I'd be in my office again, and then someone knocked on the door three times—very loud," Terry demonstrated. "So, I think someone is dropping something off. I get up and immediately run to the door. I don't see anybody there, so I open the door and go out, and there was no one there. I'm thinking it's kids pulling a prank. I close the door and then within a half an hour it begins again. I'm thinking it's kids. I go over, I open up the door, there's nobody there," she continued. "Now I go out the gate, look, there's nobody there. I walk around. There is no way for them to get out into the courtyard area. There's nobody there. So that happened a number of times. Then it got to the point that I refused to answer it. 'You can knock all you want.' Now I'm just annoyed. It happened three, maybe four times tops, and now it hasn't happened anymore."

Terry's stories continued. "The next thing happened in the model room. You can hear people walking, and you hear a little bit of whispering, like you hear somebody…a conversation, someone speaking but you can't make out what it is, and it's very low. When that would happen, I would just say, 'That's it. Pack it up,' and we'd leave.' I'd say [to the spirits] 'You guys have your fun.'"

Other incidents that occurred in the building had to do with the security system, specifically with the motion sensors. On at least three occasions, the motion sensors would set off the alarm in the middle of the night. The alarm call goes directly to Terry's cell phone. She lives in Sayville and would jump out of bed and meet the police at the museum. Each time, there was absolutely no explanation about what set them off. No one had broken into the building, and nothing had been touched.

The last story Terry told us had happened more recently, during one of the most popular events, the annual Halloween boat burning:

Each year at the boat burning, someone donates a boat that is beyond repair. They are typically Chris-Crafts, thirty-six, forty-five-foot boats. We block them up on land, close to the beach, and then it's an event. It's a bonfire. During the 2019 boat burning, a high school student took photos and donated them to the museum and then we put them on the website. When he sent me the photos, I was going through them quickly. I'm looking at them in a small view [on the computer], *and I'm working on the website to lay*

In the smoke is the profile of a sailor's head above the firemen standing on the left side. *Photo by Ryan Sweezy.*

them out. All of a sudden, I see a face in one. I'm looking at these beautiful, dynamic, fiery photos that are magnificent. I lay them all out and put them all up and then I go to one of our staff members and said to her, "Erin, look at the website, it looks great." So, she pulls it up, and I told her to look at all the photos, and she scrolls down, and she gets to this one photo, and she says, "Oh my God!" And there it was, the face of a sailor. When we got copies of the photos a few days later we saw the face. It is right over the group of firemen that are standing next to the fire. It's clear as day. It's really amazing. I was so shocked by it. I called the boy's dad and said to him, "You need to take a look at this photo." I don't know how he didn't notice it. He pulled the image up on his phone and he was like, "Wow!" It is a man's face. He has on a sailor's head scarf or bandana. He's in profile so you can see his hair sticking out. What was weird was that after that event, when I came back to the building to lock up, I had such a feeling of fear. Just in this room. I can't describe it. I just want to say fear, and I've never had that here.

I did not want to interrupt Terry while she was telling us her riveting stories, but finally, I had to say something.

"The whole time we have been in the room I've had a feeling on my left-hand side. A cold, tingling feeling—cold," I said.

At that moment, Joe said, "I just saw something fleeting off our right-hand side. During the time when Terry was telling us about the trophies flying off the wall, and about the knocking, I too felt someone alongside us. It was like someone's presence was there watching us."

At one point Joe and I both heard a knocking sound, and we each called it out as it happened. "A spirit-rap," said Joe.

After the interview, we conducted our investigation in the building. We did two ghost box sessions, one in the library and one in the attic. Here is a sample of what we got in the library:

Joe: All right, so let's introduce ourselves and explain what we're going to do.

Terry: I'm Terry. I'm the director of the museum.

Kerriann: I'm Kerriann, I'm writing the book.

Spirit: Ooh!

Terry: Ooh.

Kerriann: It sounded like, "Ooh."

Joe: Ooh?

Joe: And I'm Joe, the ghostbuster...

Joe: No comment, huh?

Spirit: No comment accepted.

Kerriann: How many of you are here with us?

Spirit: Hey you!

Kerriann: Hey you.

Terry: Who are you?

Spirit: Ed.

Kerriann: Ed.

Joe: Ed.

Kerriann: Ed, did you live here?

Spirit: I lived.

Kerriann: Ed, were you a captain?

Spirit: Correct!

Joe: Yes.

Spirit: Is the captain!

Joe: He is the captain.

Spirit: Which captain?

Joe: Which captain?

Spirit: Jacque, L.I.
Joe: Whoa! That was a different voice.
Kerriann: Captain on Long Island?
Kerriann: You're a captain on Long Island.
Spirit: Midshipman.
Kerriann: Are you the one that knocks the trophy off the shelf?
Spirit: We knocked.
Group: We knocked. We knocked.
Kerriann: Did you hear that?
Joe: We knocked. There's more than one.
Kerriann: Why do you knock off the trophies?
Spirit: I shouldn't.
Joe: I think he said, "Shouldn't."
Spirit: Hey.
Joe: Hey.
Joe: Ed, or whoever's here to use this. You just—
Spirit: Ed is.
Joe: Yeah, Ed.
Kerriann: Ed, are you the one that messes with the security system?
Spirit: It messes me.
Joe: How many spirits are here?
Spirit: Five.
Joe: Five.
Spirit: Thirty.
Joe: Thirty.
Joe: Talk louder, guys.
Spirit: Call for us.
Kerriann: Call for us.
Joe: We're getting a lot of answers.

Before we went up to the attic, Joe tried to take a photo of me and Terry in the library. For some reason, when he tried to take the photo, he couldn't press the camera button down, and his photo preview started showing timestamp information on the viewfinder. At the same time, Joe heard spirit voices talking but couldn't make out what they were saying. After a minute or two, he was finally able to snap the photo.

While we were walking around the attic, I was taking still photos while Joe was taking video. As we made our way back to the staircase to head down, Joe exclaimed, "I just captured an orb on video in the stairwell." He played

A photo taken by a ghost, as Joe captures the occurrence on video.

it back, and sure enough, he did. At this point, Terry was called away to receive a phone call, and she told Joe and me that we could walk around the building and that she would catch up with us for the outside tour. Joe and I went around looking at all the interesting collections, all the while taking photos and video. Eventually, we made our way back to the library. Terry had not yet returned. We opened the library door and closed it behind us. No one else was in the room. I walked around silently snapping more photos. Joe was seated and he was videotaping me. I lowered my camera and was holding it, cradling it in my arms, while I took a minute to look around the room. All of a sudden, my camera, a Nikon D80, started taking photographs on its own. I was surprised the minute it went off, and I changed how I was holding it, thinking I had accidentally hit the shutter button. When I lifted the camera up, my finger nowhere near the shutter, the camera took three more photos on its own. Joe captured the incident on video.

Who is it that haunts the Long Island Maritime Museum? Could it be the ghost of an old sea captain? The Hards' chauffeur? Florence? Her husband Anson? For now, the strange happenings that have taken place there remain a mystery.

12

THOMPSON HOUSE

SETAUKET

T he Thompson house, located on North Country Road in East Setauket, was built circa 1709 and was the home to five generations of Thompsons. Listed in both the New York State and National Register of Historic Places, this five-room saltbox farmhouse was one of the largest houses in its day in the town of Brookhaven.

John Thompson, a blacksmith, came from Oyster Bay to Setauket in 1692 with his wife, Mary, and they lived in a house near the Village Green. All of the Thompson descendants come from John's lineage. His son Samuel, who was a farmer, built the house where all the future generations of Thompsons would live. He lived there with his wife, Hannah Brewster, daughter of Reverend Nathaniel Brewster, and their children. Samuel's son Jonathon took part in the Revolutionary War and died in 1786. He is buried at the Thompson family cemetery located behind the house up on a hill.

Jonathon's son, who he named Samuel after his father, was the great-grandchild of John Thompson and was probably the most well-known of all the Thompsons. Samuel, born in 1738, was a farmer, a doctor of medicine, a captain in the Revolutionary War and a prestigious leader in Setauket. His land and farm extended from Setauket to Middle Island and to Old Field Point. Samuel oversaw the daily workings of the farm, but he did have servants, slaves and family members to help run it. At the same time, he was also known as the town doctor and saw patients at his house and made and dispensed medicine. He was affiliated with many patriotic causes, including being a leading member of the Committee on Safety, which was organized and developed in Brookhaven in 1776. Its purpose was for members to monitor their neighbors' activity to make sure they were not being disloyal to the Patriot cause. Samuel was also involved in protecting and surveying Setauket and Stony Brook harbors against the British troops and their possible invasion. His job included making sure the harbors were heavily armed, as well as providing detailed maps for Congress on the harbors' layout for the arrival of additional support troops. At some time during the war, Dr. Thompson and other Long Islanders from Brookhaven fled to Connecticut as refugees because of their "anti-British sympathies." Samuel did in fact return to Setauket and continued with his medical practice.

Some of Dr. Thompson's patients, whose names were written in his patient journals, were members of the Culper Spy Ring and included Abraham Woodhull, Austin Roe and Benjamin Talmadge. It is said that Samuel had taken a great interest in espionage and read several books on the topic. He also wrote about it in his journals. It has long been speculated that Dr. Samuel Thompson might have been involved in the spy ring, but there has been no information to prove this.

Because of Dr. Samuel Thompson's involvement in the American government and the patriotic cause, he was awarded one thousand acres of land at the end of the war. He eventually sold a parcel of this land back to the U.S. government for the construction of the Old Field lighthouse.

As for his family life, Samuel was married twice, first to Phoebe Satterly and then to Ruth Smith. He had six children with Phoebe and three with Ruth. Samuel died in 1811 and is buried with both wives in the Thompson cemetery. One of Samuel's sons, Benjamin Franklin Thompson, followed in his father's footsteps and became a doctor. He was also an attorney, the assistant clerk of Suffolk County, a postmaster and a well-known historian and author of *History of Long Island*, which was divided into three volumes.

Samuel's brother Isaac Thompson was also an important figure in American politics and government. Isaac was a judge, and was the owner and Lord of Sagtikos Manor in Bay Shore. It was Isaac who invited General George Washington to stay at the manor as his guest during Washington's tour of Long Island, where Washington thanked the people for their wartime efforts. Isaac was married to Mary Gardiner, a member of the prominent Gardiner family and descendant of Lion Gardiner of Gardiner's Island.

As for the Setauket house, several generations of Thompsons lived there, with Mary Thompson, granddaughter of Dr. Samuel, being its last resident. After her death in 1885, the house fell into disrepair. Eventually, a local farmer purchased it and housed migrant workers there. In 1943, Ward

Melville and his wife purchased the house and restored it. By 1951, the Melvilles had given the house and property to the Stony Brook Community Fund, which is now the Ward Melville Heritage Organization.

Today, the house is preserved as a historic house museum and is listed in the National Register of Historic Places. The original saltbox house was built circa 1709, as mentioned, and the addition to the south side was added circa 1800. Architecturally speaking, the house is a rectangular timber frame, two-story building with a one-story wing. It features a steeply pitched, asymmetrical gable roof with a central brick chimney. It is believed that the addition was a preexisting structure that is as old, or possibly older than, the Thompson house. The museum represents how the Thompson family would have lived in 1748. The furnishings are not Thompson pieces, nor are they original to the house, but they accurately portray the lifestyle of how a Long Island farming family would have lived during the mid-eighteenth century.

Joe and I were invited by Gloria Rocchio, president of the Ward Melville Heritage Organization, to conduct an investigation at the Thompson house, which we did in November 2017. While we were doing our walk-through of the various rooms in the house, Joe and I encountered some paranormal

Thompson House.

Orbs in the attic.

Close-up of an orb in the attic.

Double orb in the older part of the house.

activity. A door on the main floor closed when we were not near it, and an abundance of orbs of various sizes were photographed upstairs in the attic area, some of which were captured in motion. The smaller attic area above the circa 1800 addition also showed a number of orbs. In one photo they can be seen on and around Joe.

Our ghost box recordings revealed some short correspondence with the spirits. We could not ascertain whether or not they were members of the Thompson family. Here is some of the conversation from our transcript:

> *Joe: Hi, spirits. How are you doing?*
> *Spirit: Hi.*
> *Joe: Hi!*
> *Joe: Alright, spirits, you want to help us? We're at the Thompson house.*
>   *You know that?*
> *Spirit: Thank you.*
> *Joe: You're welcome.*
> *Spirit: Who cares?*
> *Joe: Who cares? We do!*

Kerriann: Do you like this area?
Spirit: All of them!
Joe: That was an answer!
Spirit: Presently.
Joe: We're going to walk down the stairs. We're in the attic right now.
Spirit: Hello.
Joe: Okay, so we're back in the dining room, aka surgery room, aka meeting room.
Joe: How are you today?
Spirit: Fine.
Joe: Kerriann is here. You want to say hello to Kerriann?
Spirit: Hiya!
Joe: Hiya.
Spirit: Hi.
Joe: Okay, those are…greetings.
Kerriann: Okay. Your question—
Joe: Question for you spirits.

Joe surrounded by orbs.

Spirit: No problem.
Joe: No problem.
Kerriann: Was Abraham Woodhull and Austin Roe in this house during
*   the Revolutionary War?*
Spirit: All dead.

Although the Thompson house was not as "active" as some of the other places investigated in this book, the body of evidence suggests the Thompson house has a good number of spirits from the past and historical energy trapped in its walls.

Today, the Thompson house remains a shining example of Setauket's history and will continue to be visited and enjoyed by generations to come.

13

OLD BURYING GROUND

SAG HARBOR

Sag Harbor is truly a wonderful town rich in history, and I was anxious to find a ghost story there. During my research, I came across an article written a few years back about a haunted walking tour of the village. The tour was given by the editor of the *Sag Harbor Express*, Annette Hinkle, and former history teacher turned historian Tony Garro. Their event, just in time for Halloween, was very well received as they explored ghostly locales. In addition to the haunted tour, Garro also offered a walking tour of the Old Burying Ground, which is steeped in history. There was something about the cemetery that seemed to intrigue me, so I decided to pursue it.

I contacted Tony Garro to see what I could find out, and he was delighted to speak with me. When he retired around 1996, Tony and his wife decided to move out to Sag Harbor after having lived most of their married life in Nassau County. Tony immediately took an interest in the town's history and came up with the idea of doing a history hike.

"The more research I've done in Sag Harbor, the more incredible [the history] becomes," Garro said to me during a phone interview.

"The amazing thing about Sag Harbor is the richness of its history," he continued. "It was a bustling town during the whaling industry and then it was a manufacturing town for a while. There are a lot of old houses around that were owned by whaleship members and captains, and they were huge houses. Once the whaling industry collapsed, many of these houses became boardinghouses."

Tony began giving walking tours of these historic places over twenty years ago. As his tours evolved, he started hearing from the people on the tour who'd tell him they'd heard that some of the houses were haunted.

"When people would tell me that a house had a ghost I would say to them, 'Oh! Do tell!' and they'd tell me stories. That piqued my curiosity, so I started digging into Sag Harbor's spectral history, and that's how the haunted tours began," said Garro.

The Old Burying Ground is located on Union Street off Madison and was once part of a heavily wooded area. Adjacent to the cemetery is the Old Whalers' Church, which was the tallest structure on Long Island for nearly ninety-four years, until the hurricane of 1938 blew off the 185-foot-tall steeple. When it fell, it landed next door in the Old Burying Ground. Wealthy ship owners, captains, church members and local businessmen came together to support the building of the Presbyterian church in 1842. It was officially dedicated in 1844.

"The Old Whalers' Church is a hotbed for ghostly happenings," said Garro. "A member of the congregation died, and the next day, he was seen attending the choir practice. That happened maybe ten, twelve years ago. There's a keeper of the church who took care of the interior of the church, and he was actually locked into the belfry of the church where the bell used

Old Whalers' Church.

to be. He knew that he left the door open and that someone locked it on him, and there was no one else in the church at the time."

Tony continued, "One of the secretaries told me that every day at three o'clock in the afternoon the phone would ring and there would be no one on the other end."

The cemetery is next to the church, but it is not a church burying ground. It is a public burying ground. When I asked Tony about the cemetery being haunted, he had not heard that it was.

"When I was doing the tours, we'd be at the church, and then we would walk through the Old Burying Ground to get to a haunted house that was located on the other side. So it sits in between two haunted properties," said Tony. "I have never heard of any ghostliness in the Old Burying Ground. It looks like it should be, but I have not come up with anything. I would be very interested in what you find."

The Old Burying Ground was formed circa 1767, with the first burials being that of two infant sons of Tory innkeeper James Howell. It is said that they were buried in unmarked graves. The cemetery was actively used for approximately one hundred years and is the resting place of over 335 people made up of Sag Harbor's early residents, the founding fathers of the village, Revolutionary War Patriots, whaling captains, Portuguese seamen and African Americans. The last person to be buried in the cemetery was Hetty Parker, who died in 1870.

When the burying ground was constructed, it was enclosed by a picket fence. Later, a stone wall was erected around the cemetery on Madison Street but was torn down in 1863. In 1880, another picket fence replaced it until a wrought iron fence was donated by the Ladies' Village Improvement Society around 1909. The fence still stands today.

During the Revolutionary War, the British came and occupied much of Long Island, including Sag Harbor. Needing an elevated piece of land to set up their fort, the British picked the burying ground that offered the best view of the harbor and approaching ships. The Redcoats cut down many of the trees and desecrated the graves, devastating the townspeople, many of whom then fled to Connecticut. It was said that Burying Yard Hill, as it was called then, was "crowned with a breastwork and a ditch, and the space within armed." Some of the outline of this ditch can still be seen on the Madison Street side of the cemetery.

In 1777, the Battle of Sag Harbor took place. This important historical event, also more commonly known as Meigs Raid, was a successful surprise attack on British forces. Prior to the raid, there had been a number of

Old Burying Ground, Sag Harbor.

discouraging losses for the Patriots during the Revolutionary War after the Battle of Long Island began. An officer from Connecticut, Lieutenant Colonel Return Jonathon Meigs, on his own accord, came up with a plan to take the British stronghold at Sag Harbor.

It was after midnight on the night of May 23, 1777, when Colonel Meigs and 130 Patriots quietly made their journey across the sound in thirteen whaleboats. They arrived on the North Fork of Long Island and then carried their boats south to Sag Harbor. After hauling their boats, Colonel Meigs divided his troops in half. One detachment went to the harbor while the others ventured off on foot to the Old Burying Ground and the British camp. In silence, they quickly moved toward the fort with fixed bayonets as the British soldiers drank and slept. It is said that only one shot was fired. During the ambush, six Redcoats were killed and fifty-three were taken captive. The Patriots who were stationed at the harbor then got into their boats and moved toward the British ships. Eventually, the British noticed the oncoming men and opened fire. The Patriots pushed onward and burned twelve British ships, destroying cargoes of rum, grain, hay and essentials. An additional thirty-seven prisoners were taken into custody, bringing the total number up to ninety. Not a single Patriot was lost.

This raid was a much needed turning point in the war. It was the only successful Patriot attack on Long Island between the British takeover in 1776 and the British departure in 1783.

General George Washington wrote a congratulatory letter to Colonel Meigs's superior officer, where he gave his sincerest thanks to Meigs. In recognition for the achievement, the Second Continental Congress awarded Colonel Meigs with "an elegant sword," which is now in a collection at the Smithsonian Institute.

On May 23, 1902, on the anniversary of Lieutenant Colonel Meigs's successful raid, the Sag Harbor Historical Society donated a granite monument to the village of Sag Harbor to honor Colonel Meigs. The impressive monument is located just east of 44 Union Street.

At least nineteen known Revolutionary War heroes are buried in the Old Burying Ground, their graves marked with American flags.

Of the 335 people buried in the old cemetery, 72 are children under the age of three years old. There are 9 children buried between the ages of four and ten, and 22 children are buried between the ages of eleven and twenty.

Sixteen-year-old Frederic Fordham, son of Captain Daniel Fordham and his wife, Phebe Jessup, followed in his father's footsteps and fought for freedom during the Revolutionary War. He was captured by the British and was sent to one of the horrific prison ships in New York Harbor. It is believed that he was kept on the prison ship for two years, living in completely deplorable conditions. When he was finally released, despite his condition, he managed to walk across Long Island back to Sag Harbor. He died two weeks later on June 25, 1782, from the ailments and abuse he endured while on the ship. He is buried at the Old Burying Ground.

In the southeast portion of the burying ground on Latham Street is an open and seemingly unused portion of the cemetery. It is here that the local Black residents of Sag Harbor were believed to be buried in unmarked graves. It is possible that wooden crosses might have been used to mark the graves at the time of the burials. Along with them were five Portuguese whaling sailors and one Portuguese child, evidence that segregation was in play among the town's minority residents. From 1798 to 1832, there were at least seventeen other documented deaths of African Americans living in Sag Harbor. Some have been marked with grave stones.

The types of stones that appear in the cemetery are made up of sandstone, slate, marble and schist. Several fieldstones can also be found in the Old Burying Ground that might have marked the site of those who were unable to afford to purchase a carved headstone. In other cemeteries across Long Island, footstones were often removed to make maintenance easier.

Not far from the Old Burying Ground is Oakland Cemetery, a public cemetery that began burying Sag Harbor's deceased residents in 1840. In

Grave of Revolutionary War patriot Frederic Fordham.

1860, 139 graves from the Old Burying Ground were removed from the Madison Street side and were reinterred at Oakland Cemetery. Concerned citizens had been worried about heavy spring rains exposing and washing the caskets down the hill and into the street.

On the day Joe and I set out to investigate the Old Burying Ground, Joe arrived first and headed up the hill to see what kinds of impressions he could get. I had not given Joe any previous information about the cemetery ahead of time. His first impression was that the cemetery was an "idyllic place to visit—a sanctuary of souls replete with the DNA of history and bravery!"

Having not yet known about the battle that had taken place there, Joe picked up the spirit of a British soldier who he believed was trying to communicate with him. Joe could sense anger and a feud between two groups of people. He also had a vision of water, like a river rushing by the embankment, and he wondered if caskets had washed away. Joe did not have any knowledge of the spring rains and the removal of the caskets. He also sensed a great number of young people buried there. Multiple times, he had a very strong feeling that a lynching had taken place in the cemetery.

On my arrival, I lugged my camera equipment up the hill and went to find Joe. As I got to the top, I stopped to look at a tree that caught my attention. The tree was oddly shaped and dead. Something made me wonder if someone had been hanged there. I mentioned this to Joe, and he told me about his initial impressions that someone might have been hanged here. We walked back to take a look at the tree when we witnessed something very odd.

"While we pondered this mysterious tree and its possible use for sending some unlucky person, via a roped ending, to the other side," Joe wrote in his investigative report to me, "a large black crow—a spiritual totem—suddenly landed on the tree and sat there like a dark sentinel, watching us. Edgar Allen Poe could not have been more pleased with this crow's arrival!"

It was very strange indeed, and I kept insisting that Joe take photos of the surrounding area. I was photographing as well, but my images did not reveal anything unusual.

A few days later I received a phone call from Joe, who told me he made a grisly discovery in one of the five photos of a tree that was very near the original tree we were photographing. In the photo, there appeared to be an apparition of a man hanging.

"I do feel this apparition is likely an illusion caused by a combination of light, shadow and background objects, such as headstones, trees, leaves and building structures," said Joe. "Whereas an orb may be visible in only one

Image of a hanging man to the left of the large tree trunk. *Photo by Joe Giaquinto.*

or two photos, even moving around at times, this image remains the same over several photos, which is why I feel it's not so much a light anomaly as it is a product of matrixing and pareidolia and me being in the right place at the right time. Does this relinquish its merit as a ghost photo? I don't believe so. There are just too many aspects of the apparition to explain it away as simply an optical illusion."

I contacted Tony Garro to see if he had ever heard of anyone being hanged in the Old Burying Ground.

"There is a rumor of a hanging during the Revolutionary War," said Tony. "There was talk about it after the war was over. Apparently, some Hessian soldiers were captured, and several were hanged on Main Street, but I never verified there were. That's the only hanging story I've ever heard."

Joe and I surmised that there very well could have been someone who was hanged in the Old Burying Ground. Joe's feeling was that it was someone accused of treason.

During our ghost box recording session, we received amazing information. Here is a portion of the communication:

> *Kerriann: Are there anyone from the British from when this was a fort?*
> *Spirit: There's one.*
> *Kerriann: Is there anyone here from the British soldiers?*
> *Spirit: Hi.*
> *Joe: He said hi.*
> *Spirit: Try me.*
> *Kerriann: Was anyone hung in this cemetery?*
> *Spirit: Two people were.*
> *Joe: Two people were.*
> *Kerriann: Yeah, that's what I thought he said.*
> *Joe: The British were on this side of the road?*
> *Spirit: Check.*
> *Joe: Check.*
> *Spirit: The fort! [British accent/music plays]*
> *Joe: The British were over here in this cemetery. This is the fort over here?*
> *Spirit: There's little doubt.*

As the spirit told us, there is little doubt that much went on in the beautiful Old Burying Ground, especially during the time of the Revolutionary War. It was a peaceful resting place for many and a place of turmoil for others, but it remains an important part of Sag Harbor's history to this day. As for the hanging man, did the horrible event really take place? The evidence we received has been presented. We leave it up to you, the readers, to decide whether or not you believe.

14

SANDS-WILLETS HOUSE

PORT WASHINGTON

I n my quest to find more haunted locations in Nassau County, I was poking around the internet and discovered the Cow Neck Peninsula Historical Society, which is located in Port Washington. This wonderful organization was formed in 1962 by a group of local residents who came together to promote local history. Their main mission is "to engage people of all ages in programs that highlight the lifestyles of the people and families that lived and worked on the peninsula throughout the years."

They maintain two historical properties: the Thomas Dodge Homestead on Harbor Road, circa 1721, and the Sands-Willets House on Port Washington Boulevard, circa 1735. There was nothing in my research that mentioned either house having any ghosts, but when I saw the dates they were built, I thought to myself, how could they not?

I decided to take a chance and give them a call. To my delight, I spoke to education director Ann Latner, who was intrigued by the idea of Joe and me coming and doing an investigation at one of the houses. After Ann cleared our visit with the president and board, Joe and I set up a date to visit the Sands-Willets House.

We met up with Ann Latner; Fred Blumlein, treasurer on the board of trustees and past president; and his wife, Pat, who is an active member and volunteer. Ann has been the education director since January 2020, and she was a trustee for a decade before that. Fred and Pat have been involved in the society since 1995. They proved to be a wealth of information on both the history of the area and about the house, which they are very proud of.

"We have periodic exhibits [here] and we open the house for house tours from May through October," said Ann. "We also have historic walking tours in town, and we have a fall fair that's a really big deal. That's our biggest program. We also have an open house at the Thomas Dodge house in May, and now we are starting to plan education programs. We are a growing organization."

"The Cow Neck Peninsula Historical Society starts at Northern Boulevard," said Fred. "That's where the fence was that the early settlers put up to contain their cows. That's why it's called Cow's Neck."

"There were a number of houses that were on this site," Fred continued. "The Sands family Sands Point [was named after] came here about 1690. At that time they had to have access to water, and this was wonderful since it's a peninsula. So the farm actually went out to Roslyn Harbor. All the land from here over was their land. They [the Sands family] occupied the land until about 1845, when Willets, who was a Quaker, bought the property and bought the house."

John Sands was a sea captain who was born in 1649. Along with acquiring the land the house sits on, he also purchased the land where Sands Point is. He gave approximately three hundred acres, which he called Inland Farm, to his oldest son, John Sands II. John II had been living on Block Island at the time and came back to the family homestead circa 1712. It is John II who might have built the house, or it could have been built by his son, John Sands III. Records indicate that John III did in fact live in the home. Colonel John Sands IV, the oldest son of John Sands III, became the owner of the Sands-Willets House in 1760. In 1811, the home, farm and approximately three hundred acres were passed along to John Sands V.

The construction of the home is quite interesting because it was actually built as three separate houses that were joined together. The original eighteenth-century home was a one-and-a-half-story, four-bay structure. Architectural reports reveal that the house more than likely had four rooms, each with fireplaces. A half story was located above the main floor, and there was a cellar. The room that exists today on the far west end was once an enclosed shed without windows. Much of the foundation, along with the original cellar, are still intact.

The homestead is a National Parks Service–recognized Revolutionary War site. According to Fred, seven brothers born in that house took part in the revolution in some way.

"The big hero was John Sands IV," said Fred. "He was a colonel of the local militia, the Cow Neck Manhasset Bay Great Neck Militia. In fact, they

Sands-Willets House.

were Minutemen. They were called up during Washington's invasion of New York, after Boston. Washington's army was in Brooklyn, and the Battle of Brooklyn Heights took place. Washington escaped at night through the fog, and they went across to Manhattan. John Sands actually returned home at that particular point because the British were taking over Long Island. He was captured here, and he had some money and bailed himself out. But he escaped to Washington's army across the Sound to New Rochelle. There's a story about his wife, which is wonderful," continued Fred. "He [John Sands] got a note back to her that there was ammunition—powder and shot—in the house here, and basically, she got in a boat and went across the sound and dropped it off to him. She actually came back, but she had to escape very quickly because they [the British] were after her too. She eventually wound up back with her husband in Westchester County. All the brothers were involved in the fight for independence, and many went on to become congressmen, bankers and so on. So there is a rich heritage that comes from the Sands family."

In 1838, John Sands V started selling off large portions of his Inland Farm and, in 1842, sold 211 acres of land to Edmund Willets. Edmund was a prominent Quaker and successful New York City businessman operating E&J Willets & Company, importers and wholesale dealers of fine crockery. His company was the first importer of fine crockery in the United States.

Elizabeth Sands, the unmarried daughter of John Sands, was the last member of the Sands family to live in the house. In 1846, Willets acquired the Sands house and an additional eighteen acres of land from Elizabeth's estate. As an addition to the small Sands house, Willets excavated an extensive cellar adjacent to it and moved a large Greek Revival–style half house onto the east end of the new foundation. This half house had been moved from somewhere else on Long Island. By 1850, he had built a matching half to his home and connected the old Sands house to the new Willets building.

He then had another Greek Revival–style structure built, similar to the half house, which was constructed over the open cellar and was built between the two buildings. The three houses were then converged into one. The fireplaces on the east end of the Sands house were demolished, and Greek Revival–style front and rear porches with Doric columns were added. Willets renamed the homestead Homewood.

In 1882, Edmund's son Thomas Whitson Willets inherited the home and property. On Thomas's death, his daughters, Anna Willets Lapham and Eliza Keese Willets, became the new owners, and they continued to run the property as a working farm until around 1920. There were many changes made to the house during the time the Willets family occupied it. In 1967, Eliza Willets sold the house to the Cow Neck Peninsula Historical Society, and the house has been going through renovations ever since. The Sands-Willets house has eighteen rooms, eleven that are furnished and open to the public. The colonial kitchen remains as the oldest portion of the house.

"We have a mixed bag of furnishings here that actually came from Cow Neck," said Fred. "Everything you see here, everything but the display cases, were given to us by families on the Neck, which is really interesting. So the furnishings are interesting, no question about it, but the intent of our tours is really talking about the families and the relationship of human beings who occupied the space."

Behind the house is a colonial garden that dates from 1680 to 1840 and a large circa 1690 Dutch barn that came from one of the original Sands Farms in Sands Point. It is one of only three Dutch barns left on Long Island. It came to the society in 1978, when a community barn raising took place. The barn currently houses a large antique tool collection.

Nearby is the Sands Cemetery, located on private property in Sands Point, which the Cow Neck Peninsula Historical Society also maintains. It is here that John Sands I and his wife, Sybil Ray Sands, are buried.

Once we had the history of the house down, our conversation turned to the possibilities of spirits roaming the home. Neither Fred nor Pat had ever experienced anything unusual in the house, and neither did Ann, although she did relay the following to us: "I will say this. I was talking to the president, Chris, and he said to me that just the other day he saw what seemed to be a person out of the corner of his eye, and it walked across the room. And he said the hair on the back of his neck stood up, and he went and looked all around, but there was nobody there."

Ann, Fred and Pat were definitely interested to find out if any spirits were in the house. As we did our tour, I took lots of photos with two cameras. We started with the older part of the house and worked our way around. When we got to the circa 1835 half house section in the front parlor, there was a portrait of Edmund Willets, and I took several photographs. In one of the photos, an orb appeared very close to the portrait. We continued our tour, making our way down the hall and to the upstairs bedrooms. It wasn't until I got home and went through all of my photographs that I discovered several other orbs in various locations in the house. One appeared in the middle room, in the older section of the house, on the left side of the mantle over the kitchen hearth. I had revisited this area after we completed the house tour and took more photos of the hearth. Again, in one of the photos was an orb, this time just below the mantle over the hearth. Could this have been John Sands or his wife?

Portrait of Edmund Willets with orb on the wall above the Victrola.

In the center hall across from the front entrance I captured several orbs. One very distinct orb appeared on the information board on the wall, and six other smaller and fainter orbs appeared above the board, on the wall and on the ceiling. Lastly, a small orb appeared on the floor of an upstairs bedroom.

I did not know about the first orb by Willets's portrait until I decided to look at the images on my camera in the basement. The five of us were standing together, and Joe was commenting on something as I looked through the images and found the orb. I enlarged it for the group to see, and as I did so, Fred, who had never experienced anything paranormal in his lifetime, announced a sudden and icy cold feeling coming up from behind him and on his back. He was really taken by surprise, and it happened at the exact minute I had announced the orb and thought it could be Edmund Willets. The cold spot seemed to have lasted thirty seconds or more, and Fred stood very still. He was the only one in the group who felt it. He was completely amazed and extremely interested in the phenomenon.

Joe had gotten several mediumistic impressions during our walk through. In the older part of the house, he had visions of the British raiding the house in search of John Sands IV. He also saw images of upscale and prominent people milling about in the front and rear parlors of the half house. At one point, through his mediumship, Joe connected with Edmund Willets. Mr. Willets thanked us for visiting his house and asked Joe to ask the staff what they intended to do with the house preservation. He wanted to make sure the house would not be demolished. Joe then addressed these questions with the staff during our ghost box session.

The five of us gathered again in the old Willets office to see if we could connect with Edmund or any other spirit willing to talk with us. Here is a portion of our recorded session:

Joe: Hi, spirits. How are you?
Spirit: We're fine.
Ann: I thought I heard him say fine?
Joe: Fine, right? OK, make a note of that.
Joe: If you hear anything, just call it out.
Spirit: Fine.
Joe: Did you hear them? They said it again. Just to validate it.
Spirit: You got me?
Joe: Yeah, that was a loud one fine.
Spirit: That's right.
Joe: Thanks, spirits!

Spirit: Yazoo.
Joe: Hi, spirits. How are you?
Spirit: Present.
Spirit: I am free!
Kerriann: I'm Kerriann.
Spirit: Thank you!
Ann: I'm Ann.
Pat: I'm Pat.
Fred: I'm Fred.
Joe: I'm Joe.
Spirit: Good evening, sir.
Joe: Good evening. Who's here today? Give us your names.
Spirit: Oh, dear!
Kerriann: This is Kerriann. How many spirits are visiting with us today?
Spirit: One.
Group: I heard one. I heard one also.
Kerriann: Mr. Willets, I took a photograph of your portrait.
Spirit: You did?
Kerriann: Was that you with the orb? [A humming vibration sound
   was then heard.]
Kerriann: Was that your spirit next to your portrait?
Spirit: Perhaps, you're right.
Kerriann: Yeah, right I think he said?
Spirit: What's your name?
Group: What's your name?
Kerriann: I heard that too.
Joe: Yeah.
Kerriann: My name is Kerriann.
*Kerriann: Mr. Willets, were you with us in the basement? Were you next
   to Fred?*
Spirit: You got him. He's my friend.
*Fred: Mr. Willets. This is Fred. Your house is in good hands. We try to
   maintain it as best we can, and we will continue to do so in the future.*
Spirit: We like it!
Joe: Thank you to the spirits. Thank you, Mr. Willets, for talking to us.
Spirit: Good luck, sir!

Ann, Fred and Pat were in awe of our session, and we all concluded the
spirit we were communicating with, in our opinions, was Edmund Willets.

We based this conclusion on the body of evidence we collected and the phenomena that took place during our investigation at the house. We all determined that the energy in the house is positive and peaceful and that the spirits in general are content and happy that the house has been restored.

We said our goodbyes to Fred and Pat and then Joe and I ventured outside to tour the grounds and the Dutch barn with Ann. When we had arrived a few hours before, it was gray and raining. By the time we toured the property, the sun was shining and there was a beautiful blue sky. I smiled, thinking the spirits were happy with our visit.

The Sands-Willets house is a Village of Flower Hill Historic Landmark and is listed in the State and National Registers of Historic Places and is featured as a historic site on the New York State Revolutionary War Heritage Trail. The Cow Neck Peninsula Historical Society continues to lovingly maintain and operate the Sands-Willets house as a public museum, educational center and exhibition venue for future generations.

15

SLAVE BURIAL GROUND

STONY BROOK

A few years back, Joe and I were giving a lecture on the Brewster and Thompson houses for the Ward Melville Heritage Organization in Stony Brook. After our presentation, Joe and I sat down to sign copies of *Historic Haunts of Long Island*, when we were approached by a man who wanted to speak with us. His name was Bob McCarroll, owner of the Good Steer restaurant in Lake Grove and a Stony Brook resident.

McCarroll, having learned about our interest in genre painter William Sidney Mount, told us that he happened to have his own unexplained experiences with Mount. He also told us that some of the Hawkins-Mount family slaves were buried in his backyard. I put my book-signing pen down and looked up at him, intrigued by the information he just provided. We got to talking and then he handed me his business card and said, "If you decide to write another ghost book, give me a call."

At the time, I was working on *Historic Crimes of Long Island*, and I had no idea if another ghost-related book was in my future, but I held on to his card. When the time came that I was writing this, my fourth historic ghost book, I gave him a call. He remembered our meeting, and he and his wife, Anna, agreed to give me an interview. The interview took place during the height of the coronavirus pandemic, and it was the first time Joe and I conducted an interview via Zoom. It wasn't until months later, with masks and social distancing in play, that we were finally able to go to the McCarrolls' house and see the graves for ourselves.

Bob, a longtime Stony Brook resident, had purchased his home, which is around the corner from William Sidney Mount's house, in 1989. The house as it stands now was built in 1937. There is evidence that a previous house, possibly dating back to 1790, once existed there. There are remnants of a foundation from "a very old house," as Bob puts it. He has tried to find out about the history of the house, but little is known about it. There are stories surrounding it that are unsubstantiated, but Bob has an inkling that they might be true. He had heard that the earlier house apparently burned and that during Prohibition there was a still set up in it. During the 1930s, a new house was put on the old foundation, and one of the walls appears to be original. The neighborhood where his house is located consisted of summer bungalows that were built during the 1930s and early 1940s.

There is a rare book called *Stony Brook Secrets* (1942) by historian Edward A. Lapham. There is a chapter that spoke about the slave graves and about the original house. Lapham wrote:

> *I remember several years ago answering a fire alarm from a little house on the south side of the train tracks. The bank hides it from my view, but it is just a stone's throw away. It is an old house also, built about 1790. A chimney fire had broken out between floors. The house was saved and partly cleaned, for each fireman carried off as much soot as his body and clothes would accommodate. It is deserted at present, with windows broken, stoop gone and roof sagging. At one time a piano maker lived here; he worked in Seabury's factory, which was on the hill a short distance west.*

In this same chapter, he wrote about the graves. It is unknown whether another house was built from 1790 to around 1930, when the bungalow was built. When Bob purchased it, it had been one story with two bedrooms downstairs. The two original bedrooms still exist. Bob had expanded the house by building a second floor with two additional bedrooms, and he blew out the back of the house to accommodate a larger living room. Bob explained that the property on which the house sits was once a part of the original Hawkins-Mount homestead and that from his property the tops of the Mount house barns can be seen.

The McCarolls own a little more than a half-acre of property, but directly behind their lot is another three acres of wooded land that is owned by the state and surrounds the Stony Brook University property. The Long Island railroad also has a route through the dense woods.

Stony Brook University was established in 1957 on the grounds of a previous Gold Coast estate in Oyster Bay. A new campus was built in 1962 near the historic village of Stony Brook on land that was donated by local philanthropist Ward Melville. It is said that, originally, the entrance to the university was to be built in the wooded area behind the McCarolls' house. When they started to clear some of the land, they found the original headstones of two Hawkins-Mount slaves named Anthony Hannibal Clapp and another simply known as Cane. Once the graves were discovered, the plans for the entrance were halted, and its present location was built. It is believed that an African American burial site is located on the three acres of state land, buried under overgrown brambles. Apparently, only a small number of historians and professors had known about the graves prior to 1962, when Stony Brook University wanted to make the entrance there.

Records indicate that in 1944, the Suffolk Museum (now the Long Island Museum) took Anthony Hannibal Clapp's headstone, which had been broken at the base, and brought it for safekeeping at the museum. In 1949, Cane's headstone was removed as well because concerned neighbors worried about vandals destroying it. A new stone marker was put in its place.

A few years back, Bob McCarroll was clearing a spot near the property border so that he could start a mulch pile. When he was digging and clearing the area, he came across the footstone to Anthony Hannibal Clapp's grave, which was not far from Cane's stone that had been replaced. As Bob

The new stone for Cane.

Stones for Mary Brewster and Anthony Hannibal Clapp.

continued clearing the area, he made another remarkable discovery. He found a third tombstone, this time of a woman named Mary Brewster. It was right there alongside the other graves and was broken into several pieces.

For Bob to unearth this stone was surely an amazing discovery. It is unclear what possible connection Mary Brewster had to the Hawkins-Mount family, but we do know that Cane and Hannibal Clapp were servants to the Hawkins-Mount family members. Not much is known about Cane except that he was one of the last slaves owned by the family and was a religious man of Christian faith. He was born on December 27, 1738, and died on January 12, 1814, at age seventy-seven. It is unlikely that he was free at the time of his death. Apparently, there is a built-in bench next to the fireplace in the Mount house that is referred to as Cane's seat for reasons unknown. Cane's original tombstone was large and marked with a lengthy epitaph that is believed to have been written by a family friend from Setauket, Ruth Smith, though other sources claim Micah Hawkins, the uncle of William Sidney Mount, wrote it. He was fond of both Cane and Clapp.

Anthony Hannibal Clapp, although a slave, was a beloved friend to the Hawkins-Mount family, especially to William Sidney Mount. As a child, William referred to Clapp as Tony or Toney. Clapp was a happy man of many talents and was known to entertain the family as well as their guests.

Anthony Hannibal Clapp was a musician and played the fiddle, sang and danced. He also taught the Mount children how to make whistles and flutes. He was born in Horseneck, Connecticut, on July 14, 1749. He came to Setauket in 1779 and died at age sixty-seven on October 12, 1816. It is said that Micah designed the gravestone for Tony, and on it was a relief of a violin, carved by Phineas Hill, a stone carver from Huntington.

After Tony's death, William Sidney Mount would often visit Tony's grave. In his journals, William wrote how he often walked through the former slave burial ground located on the family farm and as a young child "liked to hear him play his jigs and hornpipes."

It is said that at some point, when Clapp's stone had broken off, William took it back to his studio on the top floor of his family home. It was unusual at the time for the Hawkins-Mount family to memorialize two former slaves in such detail. William's brother Shepard Alonzo Mount immortalized the burial ground in a famous oil painting called *The Slave's Graves*, which he painted circa 1850. In the painting, Cane's and Clapp's tombstones are pictured next to one another behind a wooden fence and bordered by trees and a green pasture. This would indicate that the area, which is now wooded, was once an open field. Shepard's unsigned painting remains today as part of a collection at the Long Island Museum.

The graves of Cane, Clapp and Mary Brewster are not the only interesting facets of the McCarroll property. There is an old road that leads into the woods behind the graves. Known as Old Colonial Road, the remaining fragment was in common use until 1873. Prior to that, on April 23, 1790, President George Washington and his entourage traveled through the area after he visited with spy ring member Captain Austin Roe at the Roe Tavern in Setauket. Could the energy of George Washington remain among the woods?

As Joe and I walked the wooded property, strolled by the old road and visited the graves, Joe's impression was that a medley of energy was apparent and that there were several imprinted layers of history and living energy from the past, with each location on the property having a different story to tell.

As we toured the property with Bob and Anna, we picked five different areas to do our ghost box recording sessions. One of our best sessions was recorded toward the back of the property, not far from the graves, where six to eight spirits, including possibly William Sidney Mount, came through. Here is the transcript from that recording:

Spirit: Yeah, Joe?
Joe: Hi spirits, can you hear us? Yes or no.
Spirit: Yes.
Joe: I think I heard yes.
Spirit: Just as well.
Joe: Alright, you want to introduce ourselves?
Kerriann: I'm Kerriann.
Spirit: Kerriann.
Bob: I'm Bob.
Spirit: Bob.
Anna: I'm Anna.
Spirit: Anna.
Kerriann: How many spirits are with us, right now?
Spirit: Eight.
Spirit: There's about six ghosts.
Kerriann: Is William Sidney Mount with us?
Spirit: Would be!
Joe: Would be.
Kerriann: Did you hear that? Would be.
Kerriann: Is Cane with us?

The wooded trails behind the McCarroll property, where President George Washington might have passed through.

Spirit: Let's do it!
Joe: He said let's do it.
Spirit: I am!
Joe: I am! Did you hear him say I am?
Kerriann: Are you happy we're writing your story in the book, so people know that you're here?
Spirit: I'm just working.
Joe: Cane!
Spirit: Yes.
Bob: Is anybody who's familiar with the area?
Spirit: Oh, sure!
Spirit: Who can find a spy?
Spirit: McCarroll, hi!

In our previous phone interview, before our visit to the property, I asked Bob if he had heard anything about the property or house being haunted. He replied no, but he did claim that he started experiencing things almost immediately after moving in.

"There were a lot of noises and shadows," Bob began. "As soon as we kind of got comfortable with each other [the spirits], things started happening. Outside, garbage cans would be stacked on top of each other. Lights would go on and off. I'd be sitting at the table eating my dinner and the light would go off, and I would just say, 'Come on already,' and they would turn the lights back on. It was a very active place to live. It's weird because when I originally bought the house there was no second floor, but I used to hear rumblings in the attic. When I added the second floor, there was a lot of banging around upstairs, and we still hear some of it to a degree."

Anna added, "When we moved in, I would be downstairs, and Bob would be at work, and I would hear—it was like somebody had knocked down a stack of boxes. Also, heavy things, like the sound of furniture being moved. I'd run upstairs, and there'd be nothing. Nothing was moved, nothing was happening. I'd go back downstairs and then maybe later that day or the next day I would hear the same things."

Anna and Bob's youngest son, Robert, might have had a ghostly experience when he was just a small child. When he was two years old, he would be sitting by himself laughing and talking to someone who could not be seen. When Robert was about four years old, Bob and Anna went to see an exhibit of William Sidney Mount's paintings at the Long Island Museum, and Robert was with them. As they walked around the exhibit, as soon as Robert saw the paintings of several African American fiddle and banjo players, he yelled out to his parents, "Oh wow! I know those guys!" Bob said that Robert today has no recollection of it at all.

Along with noises being heard in the house, apparitions have also been seen both inside and outside of the house.

"In the front room I've seen an image of a woman who's dressed in a long dress with a white apron and a white bandana on her head, and she looked like she was mad about something," said Anna. "She was there for less than a second and then was gone. In that same exact spot, I told Bob that I've seen a man with black pants, a black long coat and a black hat."

Bob laughed and said, "Guess who that could be?" referring to William Sidney Mount, who very often dressed in that fashion.

"I've felt his presence, and I've seen him in the same place that Anna has seen him, which is where that old remaining part of the house is," said Bob.

There is another area of the house that Bob believes might be some sort of portal or vortex—the staircase that he built to go up to the second floor. Anna would wake up around the same time between 3:00 and 3:30 a.m. to the sound of voices, to people talking. She would hear it as she went down the stairs. She assumed someone had left the television on, but when she got to the bottom of the stairs, the living room was dark, no television was on and all of the children were asleep in their rooms.

"Years this was happening—years," Anna said. "The staircase…it's just like voices. You hear people talking, laughing, a staticky noise also. I can hear it in the staircase and then I go downstairs and there is no sound. It's always at night. Always around that same time. The noises now have kind of subsided."

As for the outside, Bob and Anna have seen orbs flying around the backyard on many an occasion, and they have also seen a ghostly couple every year around the end of April or May.

"I see them in white," said Anna, "and I see little kids dressed in white also, and they're running around. I always see them adjacent to the house."

"The sense I get from that," said Bob, "is that it's connected to something like a wedding. It's been happening every year for as long as I've been here. Twilight, dusk is usually when we see them."

"There is a type of ghost, a recurring or cyclic ghost where spirits can appear in regular cycles, usually annually to where the event took place," I said. "They appear at the same time every year. It could also be an atmospheric or mental image ghost where events can imprint themselves in or on the atmosphere of the place or area where the events occurred."

Could this matrixed image be the woman with the apron who Anna saw? *Photo by Joe Giaquinto.*

"Agreed. There are two types of apparitions or spiritual encounters," added Joe. "One is an imprint or place memory, place centered, which is the recurring spirit Kerriann mentioned, and the other one is ascension beings, like us, it's not leftover energy in the atmosphere, instead they are spirits or souls of people who are trying to give you a message."

The McCarroll house and property is a peaceful and spiritual place where a multitude of spirits have gathered. In reflecting back on our day there, Joe could not sum it up any better.

"All in all, I felt the day at the McCarroll property was an interesting one, replete with a smorgasbord of spiritual energy, ghost sightings and a fascinating history to glue everything together."

16

NATHANIEL CONKLIN HOUSE

BABYLON

In the quaint village of Babylon there exists a hidden gem full of history and full of spirits. Located on Deer Park Avenue, just around the corner from the bustling town, a stately Federal-style home with Victorian features appears not far from the railroad tracks. The house, known as the Nathaniel Conklin House, was moved to its present site from Main Street in 1871. It survives as "the oldest, intact landmark of its kind in the village."

Babylon was originally part of Huntington and was known as Huntington South. Huntington as we know it today was settled in 1653. Early settlers followed what they called the "Old Indian Path" to the south end of the island near the Great South Bay. The area, known as Sumpwams, was inhabited by Native Americans. When the English settlers arrived, they found much-needed salt hay that was used as food and bedding for livestock, along with an abundance of fish. By 1689, many of the settlers began making their homes on the south shore.

In 1710, Jacob Conklin built a beautiful farm home in an area called Half Way Hollow Hills, which was in Wheatley Heights. The house was destroyed by fire in 1918, but a family burial plot remains. Apparently, Jacob Conklin had acquired a bit of wealth rather quickly. It is said that he served with the infamous pirate Captain Kidd, but there are two versions of the story. The first is that he was captured and taken away to work on Kidd's vessel and then escaped. The other story was that Jacob Conklin was a "willing member of the crew" who enlisted and was a commanding officer. Whatever the case may be, the newfound family fortune was passed down through generations of Conklins who became wealthy landowners.

Jacob had married a woman by the name of Hannah, and they had seven children together. Many of the Conklins had owned property in Dix Hills. One of their sons, Platt Conklin, was a Revolutionary War soldier and was the Town of Huntington supervisor for nearly twenty-seven years. Platt and his wife, Phebe Smith, had one son, Nathaniel, who was born in 1768. Nathaniel inherited land in both Huntington and Islip. When Nathaniel was twenty-two years old, he was living in Islip and married Mary Wickham. They had two sons, William and Wickham Platt. Only four years into their marriage, Mary died in 1794. Nathaniel had owned and operated a tannery circa 1801, and it was located farther down in Huntington South. It was not easy for Nathaniel to take care of two young children and try and run a business so far away. Two years later, he decided to move closer to his work, and he would bring his widowed mother, Phebe, with him to help take care of the children. By this time, Huntington South had many taverns and inns along Main Street. Nathaniel, who had also been active in village affairs, decided to build his home on the corner of Main Street (now the northeast corner of Deer Park Avenue and Montauk Highway) in 1803, across from the American Hotel and Tavern.

Nathaniel's mother, a religious woman, was completely appalled that her son would choose to build his home and raise his family in proximity to such debauched establishments. It is said that she compared it to the biblical Babylon, the "city of sin." Nathaniel laughed and apparently said, "No, Mother, this will be the new Babylon!" and the name stuck. Nathaniel had a cornerstone carved with the name "New Babylon, This House Built by Nat Conklin 1803," which was placed on the chimney of his home. It is said that 1803 is considered the year when Babylon officially got its name. When the house was moved to its present location in 1871, the cornerstone had fallen off and was either lost or left behind. It ended up in the hands of two local sisters, Jesse and Emma Seaman. The stone was then given to a Mrs. E.V. Ketcham, who donated the stone to the new Babylon Library building, where it hung above the fireplace as a reminder of the village's history. That building became the home of the Village of Babylon Historical and Preservation Society. In 2003, the cornerstone made its way back to its rightful place in the Nathaniel Conklin house, where it is on display in a corner cabinet in the Federal Room.

A year after the house was moved, in 1872, Babylon separated from the Town of Huntington, and by 1893, the village of Babylon was incorporated.

Nathaniel Conklin died in 1844 and was buried in the Conklin family cemetery in Wheatley Heights. He had remained in the house in Babylon until around 1815, at which time he moved his family to West Islip. That same year, Nathaniel sold the house to a man by the name of Rushmore. In 1821, Phineas Carll purchased the house from Mr. Rushmore. When Phineas Carll died in 1828, he left the house to a farmer named Timothy Platt Carll and his wife. Timothy Platt Carll died in 1851. His widow decided to run a one-room general store in the house, which sold local goods as a means to augment her income. It is unknown how long she remained in the house, but records indicate that by 1871, David Sturges Sprague Sammis had bought the house as an investment. He was a very prominent figure in Babylon, and in 1851, he opened the Surf Hotel on Fire Island, which is now Robert Moses State Park. Sammis also started the horse car trolley and owned several properties.

The same year Sammis purchased the Nathaniel Conklin house he leased the house to hotelier John Lux. Mr. Lux, who was born in Germany, moved the house down the road next to the Washington Hotel, which he owned, so that it could be a part of the Depot Hotel complex. Babylon was quickly becoming a popular tourist attraction because of its proximity to the railroad, and hotels were popping up all over town. John lived in the house along with his wife, Mary, and their six children, John Jr., Casper, Edward, Colhernie, Emma and Mary. During the time Lux leased the house he modernized it by adding popular Victorian-style details. A porch was added to the front and north side of the house, a large dining room was added to the rear of the house, the front windows became full-length French windows and other decorative details were added to the interior. With these new renovations, the hotel became a popular place in the village known for its fancy balls, concerts and other forms of entertainment. A blacksmith shop and large icehouse were located on the property as part of the hotel complex.

The Lux family remained in the hotel business until 1886. Before that, in 1882, the house and property were returned to the Sammis family by foreclosure. It is unknown who lived in the house from the years 1886 to 1915. A Village of Babylon report from 1992 stated that a Mr. Charles Peratsky leased the house and ran it as a boardinghouse between 1886 and 1888; however, there is no firm documentation of this. In the same report, it states that a Mr. and Mrs. Michael Farrell ran a boardinghouse there in 1910.

Records indicate that it was a boardinghouse by 1915, run by a widow named Mary Mentz until 1930. Mary, who had five children to feed, rented rooms to local residents, salesmen and workers who were building the new Sunrise Highway.

Nathaniel Conklin House.

The Washington Hotel complex was demolished circa 1918, sometime after World War I, but the Conklin house had remained intact. On October 16, 1945, descendants of David S.S. Sammis, who still owned the house, decided to donate it to the American Red Cross. It was dedicated in memory to Antoinette Wheeler Sammis and Emeline Sammis Norton. It served as the local Babylon headquarters of the American Red Cross until 1988, at which time it was purchased for a nominal fee by the Village of Babylon, which recognized the house as an important part of the town's history. On December 8, 1988, the Nathaniel Conklin House was listed in the National Register of Historic Places.

Today, this beautifully restored, two-story, center-hall home is a museum, with the rooms in the house depicting the various time periods the house has seen. Also on the property is a magnificent garden, a replica of a carriage house at Old Bethpage Village Restoration, which was built in 1990, a small white building used as a shed and moved from another property and an outhouse that may or may not be original to the house.

Joe and I met with village trustee Robyn Silvestri; Kym Turet, member of the Conklin House Committee; and Mary Cascone, Town of Babylon historian and village resident. In addition, we had Conklin House coordinator Karen Petz on the phone with us. We sat in what they referred to as the

Orbs appear on a tree outside the Nathaniel Conklin House.

"gathering room," which was a large room not original to the house. It was added on in 1871, along with a second floor, and was a preexisting building in the area. This back area of the house is actually the oldest part of the home and predates the original 1803 building. The gathering room at one time was probably used for small business meetings, so it was apropos that our interview took place in this room.

After our initial interview, we decided to tour the house and do our investigation before the group told us of their own ghostly encounters.

"I liked the energy and the calmness of the place," Joe said to me later on. "The staff and historians were obviously dedicated and passionate about the property. This made the tour of the house even more inviting."

For the beginning of the tour, Joe and I actually separated for a bit, with me taking photos in each room and Joe using his mediumship to see what he could pick up. On the first floor in the Victorian room, Joe saw a vision of a woman in white and an older gentleman with a white beard. Perhaps Nathaniel Conklin? In the main foyer/entrance area Joe felt a lot of energy and a huge cold spot. Through his clairaudience, he heard a voice say "go" or "Joe" near the stairwell and wondered if this area could be a portal.

In the Federal Room Joe was led to the glass cabinet where the New Babylon stone was located and felt that this area, near the stone, was the spiritual heart of the house. The space was filled with energy, and Joe even commented that if a ghost was going to show up, it probably would appear here.

As he moved throughout the house, his strongest sensation was in the Red Cross room, where the temperature seemed to change drastically. In the room directly behind the Red Cross room there was a portrait of an unknown man leaning up against the wall underneath a window. All the furnishings and decorations have been gathered and donated from various locations on Long Island. None are original to the house. As for the portrait, that too was donated. Who the man in the picture is, nobody seems to know. When Joe examined the photos he took, a large swath of white, or type of ectoplasm, appeared over the man's face and body but not in the white space surrounding him in the frame. There are two theories we discussed. Since the portrait is not of someone associated with the house, perhaps the spirts who did live in the house at one time are upset the portrait is there. Or, the man in the photo could be upset that his portrait is not hung and is on the floor. In either case, this strange form appeared only in Joe's photo, not any that I took.

As for me, as I walked the house alone, I quietly took photographs and tested out the ghost meter (electromagnetic field indicator). At one point I had too much in my hands carrying around my photo equipment, so I placed the ghost meter on a bench in the entrance foyer. Leaving it on, I went into the general store to photograph. Joe and the guides were on the second floor at this point. All of a sudden from the other room, I heard the ghost meter going off. I walked out of the general store toward it and could see the red light flashing. As soon as I got near, it stopped. The same thing happened in the center hall upstairs near the front of the house. I had put the meter down on a nearby table and was photographing in a bedroom when the meter went off on its own once again.

Portrait of an unknown man blocked out by possible ectoplasm. *Photo by Joe Giaquinto.*

I then met up with Joe and the others in the Red Cross room. Without having spoken to Joe yet about his experience in the room, I immediately revealed that I had felt a huge cold spot as soon as I entered the room. Joe and the staff verified that they had felt it too.

The most interesting thing for me was when I headed back downstairs

American Red Cross room.

and went into each room with the ghost meter again. The meter went off in two places, and the signal was very strong. It was at its highest reading in the back right corner of the general store and in the center of the Federal Room and especially by the New Babylon cornerstone. The energy there was off the charts. In both rooms we ruled out any possible electrical interference. Hearing the meter going off, Joe joined me in the Federal Room and actually captured the scene on video. It was then that he had told me about the energy he felt in the room before I had gone in there. Is it possible that since the stone was lost for some time Nathaniel now stands guard over it, knowing it should always remain in the house? One can only contemplate.

There was one last area for Joe and me to see, and that was the third floor, an unfinished area of the house. We decided to go up there together and climbed the steep stairs. As soon as I got there I felt a chill and a change of energy. Joe sensed it too, along with great sadness and death. After spending only a few minutes up there, Joe had a very strong feeling that someone might have been hanged there. Joe turned to Kym and asked if anyone hanged themselves in the house, but she said she didn't know.

We made our way back to the gathering room, and we discussed our findings. As Joe and I talked, the staff looked at one another in that knowing way, anxious to now tell us about their experiences.

Federal Room with cornerstone in cabinet. Area where the ghost meter went off.

"I'm in the house quite often," Robyn began, "and I have only heard tales of other people who have said things, like feeling a young girl up in the nursery. Several people have mentioned this. On two separate occasions I've gone up to the attic on the third floor and had almost identical responses [from people] saying there is a spirit up here who does not want us up here. So I was very curious to see what your impressions were on the third floor."

We got Karen back on the phone, and she told us a few stories. "We've always heard doors slam, and it's usually more prevalent in the evening hours," Karen began.

> *I have had two experiences with different people coming into the house, and it happened months apart. I was giving a tour of the house to two women when one of the women asked the other, "Well, what do you think?" The response was, "Oh yes, there is definitely something here." I asked her what was going on, and she called herself a psychic healer. She felt something downstairs. I then said, "Let me take you to the third floor." We went up, and toward the middle of the room she got very quiet. Then she said, "We*

have to leave now. We're not welcome." She said there was not a friendly presence up there. We had always joked about someone being up there, and that was the first time someone other than ourselves felt it.

Karen continued, "A year later a ghost hunters group came and went into every room. When they got to the attic one of them said, 'No, we're not here to harm you, we're not judging you, we're friendly.' Then he said, 'Okay, we're leaving.' This happened in the same spot that the other woman explained to us that it was not a friendly presence and that something had happened there on the third floor. The ghost hunters thought somebody might have gotten killed [there]."

Another time when Karen had stopped over to bring a new piece of furniture into the house, her husband and golden retriever came along with her. The dog was on a leash and had absolutely refused to come into the house. During her time there, she and her husband heard a door slam inside when nobody else was in the house. She thought it must be Nathaniel.

Oddly enough, while we were finishing our second interview and were getting ready to conduct the ghost box recordings, Joe said he needed to go out to his car to get more batteries. When he came back he told the staff that

Three orbs appear on each of the porch columns.

there was a woman at the front door who wanted to speak with someone. Kym went to see what she wanted. When Kym came back she told us that the woman had asked if the house was open for tours. The woman said that she really wanted to come in because it was really haunted. We all laughed at the timing of this.

Our ghost box session was wonderful, and we made some great connections with the spirits. Here is a sampling:

Kerriann: Are you happy with the condition of the house?
Spirit: Yes.
Staff: Has anybody died in this house?
Spirit: Boy.
Kerriann: Is there a spirit that protects the cornerstone in the Federal Room?
Spirit: The original?
Kerriann: The original!
Kerriann: The original stone….I felt a presence. Was someone with us by the stone?
Spirit: AutoZone.
Joe: Right? Original stone—AutoZone.
Spirit: You need to add words.
Kerriann: We're going to write the history of this house in a book, to keep it alive.
Spirit: You in it?
Spirit: Good!
Spirit: Good!
Staff: Who is the woman in the Country Store?
Spirit: Poor Rose.
Joe: That was a name.
Spirit: Rose?
Spirit: Rose. It sounded like Rose.
Joe: Anybody want to chime in with a question?
Spirit: How?
Joe: The fellow upstairs—the energy in the third floor—are you here?
Spirit: It's ridiculous!
Staff: I heard that's ridiculous.
Joe: I heard that—I heard that too.
Joe: What's ridiculous? It's your situation?
Spirit: Problems.
Joe: Are you going to be okay upstairs there?

Spirit: In the room?
Staff: Are the sisters who stored the stone…in the house?
Spirit: Maybe.

A few weeks after our investigation, I called Robyn to tell her about the findings in the photograph Joe took, and she told me the following story.

Two days after you and Joe came to the house, a woman by the name of Rita came here with her daughter. They are working on a gravestone restoration project with me and wanted to see the house. They had never been inside. So, I took them on the tour and never said anything to them. Not about you coming, not about the ghosts, the book, nothing. Rita turned to me and said, "I don't want you to think I'm crazy, but has anyone ever told you there are spirts in this house?" I told her that she wouldn't be the first, then I asked what they were telling her. Apparently, her daughter was intuitive. They told me that Phebe and Ester wanted me to know that they were happy their stories are being told. Then when we got to the third floor, the daughter said, "Secret trials occurred here. Great sadness." She sensed strong energy coming from one of the wooden beams, a piece of reclaimed wood. She then said that she believed that somebody was hung here.

Since our visit, footsteps continue to be heard in the house, and lights have gone off or flickered in the Federal Room. Apparently, the spirits of the Nathaniel Conklin house are alive and well, continuing to enjoy the charm and beauty of this wonderfully preserved piece of history.

Tours and many great community programs continue at the old house for all to enjoy.

"We love this house," said Robyn. "It is truly a treasure in the village."

17

SUNDANCE STABLES PART I

MANORVILLE

I have written about and investigated over one hundred places on Long Island, and with each ghost book I have written, there always seems to be one story that has a profound impact on me. A story that stays with me. A story that makes me think. A story that reminds me how important relationships are and how the connection, even after death, is never broken.

I was introduced to Lynne and Eric Weissbard, owner of Sundance Stables in Manorville, through a mutual horse friend. Oddly enough, Joe had met them a few years back, and he begged me to write this story.

Joe and I went to the stables on a miserably rainy day in May 2019 and met up with Lynne and Eric in their home, along with two of their close friends and fellow horse people Jeanie and Gerard Leonard. There have been some unbelievable and unexplainable things that have occurred at the stable, including the sighting of apparitions, but there was more. There are actually two parts to this story. There is the story of the stable, and there is the story of Rebecca, Lynne and Eric's daughter, their only child, who died tragically in a horseback riding accident on August 31, 2016. Rebecca was only twenty-two years old and was a gifted rider. The story of Rebecca and her communication after death is so incredible that I decided she deserved to have her own chapter. Her remarkable and heartwarming story will follow this one as the last chapter in the book.

Lynne, a professional rider and trainer, and Eric, a firefighter and EMT, purchased the stable in August 2005. The property dates to 1869. It was always used as farm property and in later years as a horse stable. It currently sits on approximately fourteen acres.

Manorville at one time was a heavily forested area. Once the railroad made its way out to Manorville in July 1844, the cutting and shipping of cordwood to New York City became an important industry. It is said that at least 2,500 cords of wood were shipped from Manorville to New York City every year. Once the land was cleared, it was used for cranberry bogs and farms. The cranberry industry in Manorville lasted for one hundred years, with 25,000 bushels of blue diamond cranberries being shipped by the Long Island Railroad to New York City each year. As for the farms, asparagus was the main crop until it was overtaken by disease. From then on, farmers planted potatoes, lima beans, corn, cauliflower, cabbage, strawberries and blueberries. Today, Manorville is still considered rural and comprises residential homes, farms and horse farms.

The Weissbards' property on North Street has a private stable, several barns and pastures, an old stone well and an old root cellar, as well as the house, which Eric and Lynne have expanded over the years. Eric believes that at some time there was another house located farther back on the property, because he has found remnants of old bricks and other items.

We started getting into the ghost stories pretty quickly because Eric, originally a huge skeptic and nonbeliever, had a lot to share with us.

"I had no belief in anything like this before coming here," said Eric. "Crazy [expletive] happens. I don't consider myself a kook, but I know what I've seen. I'm not a drinker. I don't do drugs. I don't smoke anything. I'm a guy that gets up in the morning, works all day, and that's what I do."

Lynne admitted that she was always a believer but never had any prior experiences until coming to the stable in Manorville. Eric continued:

Becca [Rebecca] *was eleven when we moved here, and she would always say, "Sarah did this" and "Sarah did that." We really just thought it was an imaginary friend. One day I'm across the street talking to the fellow who lived there at the time, and just randomly, out of the blue he asks, "Does anything strange ever happen in your house?" And he was like a regular guy like me. So I said to him, "What do you mean strange?" He said, "Like things get moved, or things happen." So I tell him my daughter tells me things like that all the time, and she blames it on Sarah. And he says to me, "You know about the little girl?" I look at him and say, "What little girl?" and then he tells me that the little girl used to live in the house on the corner and that a lot of unexplained things happen around here.*

Things did in fact start moving around the Weissbard house, and strange noises could often be heard shortly after they moved into the house. Eric also felt an odd sensation every time he went down the staircase from the second floor.

"I've never had this feeling anywhere before, only here," said Eric. "Whenever I was walking down those stairs, I always felt that I was going to fall down or somebody was going to push me down the stairs. There was one time when I was coming down the stairs and I swear I saw a little girl standing right there, looking around the stairs to see who's coming. Like a kid hiding, peeking around to see who's coming down the stairs."

Another time, Eric was at a different house down the street. A welder lived there, and he was doing some work on Eric's truck. Out of the blue, the welder asked Eric if strange things happen in his house, and again, Eric was surprised by the question. The welder went on to tell him similar stories about hearing noises and items getting moved around the house. The subject of the little girl, Sarah, came up, and he had heard of her too. The welder asked for his wife to come out with a book that had the names of people who had died and who were buried in the cemetery behind their house. According to the welder, there was a little girl by the name of Sarah Raynor who was four years old when she died from falling down the stairs.

The people who had given Eric this information no longer live in the house, so I could not verify it or find out what book the information was from. Through my research, what I did find out was that there were several members of the Raynor family living in Manorville during the late 1800s. The family name goes back to the Revolutionary War and includes four Revolutionary War Patriots, Henry, Benjamin, Joseph and Josiah Raynor, each of whom are buried in various cemeteries in Manorville. There are several Raynor plots in Manorville, including the Joseph Raynor Cemetery, which is located in the woods on the east corner of North Street and Wading River Road. The *Sag Harbor Express* from September 16, 1875, lists an obituary for a Sarah Anna, the infant daughter of Gilbert W. Raynor and the late Sarah Raynor. Apparently, this Sarah died at four weeks old, not at four years old, and it did not say where she was buried. At the Joseph Raynor cemetery, there are eleven known graves, six with missing headstones. These graves are referred to as mounds. Some have rocks at each end, some none at all. Three of these mounds are six feet long, one is hard to tell how long and two others are four feet long, which indicate they could be children's graves. Could one of these graves be Sarah Raynor's, the one that Eric might have encountered on the staircase? It is very odd that Becca always referred to her "friend" as Sarah, so it is very likely that she did in fact see the ghost of Sarah Raynor. Eric admits that it's all very strange.

"Like I said before, I'm a nonbeliever," said Eric. "If I don't see things, it don't exist."

As time went on, however, more things started happening in the house, and Eric began to change his mind.

"Not long after I had the conversations with the neighbors, we had some people from down south staying in the basement, and they had a young child who was about two years old," he said. "One day the father says to me, 'If I didn't know better, I'd swear this place is haunted.' And I said to him, 'What do you mean?' He then says, 'I put the toys away, and then the toys are back out. There's no way she could have gotten out of that crib.' Then another time he told me he turned the oven off at night, and it was back on in the morning. He swore something was happening here and that someone was playing with the toys."

After the family had moved out of the basement, an army veteran studying to become a schoolteacher moved in. Within a few days of living there, he came to Eric and said that every time he leaves there is a ghost following him. Eric was not surprised, but he said that the man was petrified.

There was another person who lived in the basement, a man by the name of Paul, who was a friend of Eric and Lynne, and who had lived there for several years. Paul was in his sixties, and Eric and Lynne saw him all the time. One day Eric realized he hadn't seen Paul in a day or two, so he decided to go down to the basement to check on him. When he did, sadly, Eric discovered that Paul had died.

About two years after that I'm sitting here watching TV and I look outside, and as clear as I'm looking at you, I see who I think is Paul walking away from the house. I'm thinking what am I seeing? He had a distinct walk. He was always cold, and I used to buy him heavy jackets and things. He would always wear his hat pulled down real low and his collar up. I'm watching him walk away. I don't see anything else. So I'm thinking that was crazy! So a week goes by, and Becca comes up to me with a real serious look, and she says to me, "Dad, I have to ask you something, and I don't want you to think I'm crazy." She then said, "This is serious, and I have to talk to somebody about this." I'm wondering what it could be, and then she says, "I saw Paul. I saw Paul as clear as day." She was probably around sixteen at the time, and I said to her, "What do you mean you saw Paul?" She says, "I looked outside the house, and I saw him walking. He was wearing the coat you gave him, and he had his hat on, and he was just walking away from the house." I then said to her, "If it makes you feel better, I saw the exact same thing a couple of days ago. I thought I was crazy."

Paul wasn't the only apparition roaming the property. Eric went on to explain about another encounter:

One night during the summer, Becca was a teenager, and she asked me if she could go outside to the barn after dinner, so I said, sure. Lynne and I were talking for a couple of minutes and then I got up to put my dish in the sink and I looked out the window, and I'm watching a man walk across. I see him walk into the barn, and I didn't recognize him. I look to see if there were any cars here. I don't see any cars. I go to Lynne, "Who's that? There's some guy in the barn. Are you expecting anybody?" And she said, "No. You better go out there and see. Becca's out there." So I walk out, and the guy is wearing blue pants, a white shirt, and he walks into the barn. Becca's in the barn, her pony Lily is on the crossties, and I said to her, "Where is that man?" She says, "What man?" I said, "The man that just walked in the barn." She says, "There's nobody in the barn." I said, "I saw him. I watched him walk all the way across and walk in the barn." She then told me again that there was no one in the barn, but then she asked me how long ago it was. I told her it was as long as it took for me to get out here. A minute, two minutes maybe. She then told me that right before I went into the barn that Lily had a giant freak-out for some reason. The pony had just seen the ghost.

Eric continued, "There were several times, sitting out by the barn where we'd hear the little girl laughing. And one night it was me, Becca and her friend Liz, and it was late. They'd been out there and I went out to see what they were up to since it was midnight. Nobody lives behind us. Nobody lives for miles in any direction. Becca took whatever horse she had out and went to put it away, and I hear giggling coming from the back. I just heard giggling, and Liz looks at me and said, 'You heard that?' We all heard a little girl giggling."

There were other strange occurrences that took place over the years. Rebecca's room was always cold no matter what time of year. Another time Eric came home and found the door to the living room lying on the floor, the pins still in the hinges, and no one had been in the house. One time the

Orb at entrance to barn.

family dog went missing. It always slept with Rebecca, and one morning when Eric went to get Rebecca up for school, the dog was not there. They kept calling the dog and searched everywhere for the sheltie but could not find it. Rebecca was getting very upset. Then Eric noticed the bathroom door was closed. When he went to open it the door was locked. The door could only be locked from the inside. Eric had to pry the door open, and there was the dog standing there, shaking. There was no explanation about how the dog could have possibly gotten locked in there.

Lynne's experiences are more centered around Rebecca, which you will read about in the next chapter. We then turned our attention to Jeanie and Gerard and the paranormal experiences they had at Sundance Stables.

Gerard and Jeanie Leonard own two horses that they have boarded at Sundance Stables since 2008. Jeanie told her story first and recalled a time when she was at the stable at night by herself without Gerard. She had been a boarder there for only about four or five months, and she was new to horse ownership. She was happy that Rebecca was in the barn in case she had some questions while she tacked up her horse. After her ride, she came back, and Rebecca was no longer there.

"There was no Becca, and now it's dark out, and I'm here by myself," said Jeanie. "I didn't know any of the stories. We were new here and I was just getting to know people. So, I'm with my horse in the center barn, and it's pitch black because it's now about 8:30 p.m. I have to bring Shooter from the center barn to the barn opposite. Everything is nice and quiet, and all the horses were nodding off in the back of their stalls. I start walking Shooter, and as I start walking him past the barns, all of a sudden all the horses that are in that barn are now with their heads out of the barn, and some of them are kicking and making noises. And I'm thinking, *that's a little odd*. Anyway, so I bring Shooter into his stall and I cannot tell you," Jeanie pauses and shivers. "The feeling I had that someone was behind me. I'm thinking I'm going to turn around and there is going to be someone behind me. My whole body was tingling, the hairs on my arms were raised up. I took Shooter's halter off, shut the door and I was running. Then I realized I had to turn the light off in that barn. So, I'm running and turning the lights off, and I'm realizing it's getting darker and darker. I was so scared. Since that time I have never come here at night alone, and that was in 2008!"

Jeanie then went on to tell me how another boarder heard footsteps in the barn at night and that the same woman also saw the ghost of the little girl in the field down the road. Next we spoke with Gerard.

We were coming here on a Thursday night about four or five years ago. I worked midnights. I'm a retired police officer, and I've seen everything under the sun. I was at 9/11 for four months. I have seen the most horrific

North Street, where the ghostly figure of a Civil War soldier on horseback appeared.

things, and I've helped people make the transition when they were dying. I believe in the afterlife and all that, but I didn't think I believed in ghosts or any of that stuff. So, we were coming here on a Thursday night, and it was just about dusk, and we were coming down North Street, and I said, "This is weird…look Jeanie." So we look up and we see in the distance, coming up North Street, a horse with a male rider in a Union soldier outfit. The uniform was that grayish blue. And I'm thinking this is weird out here in Manorville on a Thursday night. Because we have horses, we know the proper etiquette, so we pull over to the side, and I let him walk by to not spook the horse. And as I did, he tipped his hat to me. He had blue eyes and blond curly hair; he tipped his hat and smiled as if he knew us, and went on his way. About fifteen seconds later, we both turned around because I didn't pull out yet, and he was gone.

Gerard continued, "I've never seen a person like that around here. I knew it was different than just someone on a horse. It was weird. You felt like he was looking right through you, and he was smiling."

"We both looked at the same time," Jeanie added, "And we said to each other, 'Did you see that?' and we're in the car and we just turned, and he was gone."

18

SUNDANCE STABLES PART II: REBECCA

MANORVILLE

Some are bound to die young. By dying young a person stays young in people's memory. If she burns brightly before she dies, her brightness shines for all time.
—Aleksandr Solzhenitsyn

The day Joe and I arrived in Manorville at Sundance Stables to interview Lynne and Eric Weissbard, we were led into a large living room where Joe and I took a seat on a couch. Across from us sat Lynne and Eric, and to my right was Jeanie and Gerard Leonard. As we settled in and I got my recorder and pad ready, I couldn't help but notice all the large photos and ribbons of Rebecca Weissbard that were lovingly placed around the room. Within a few minutes, I sensed her presence on the couch between Joe and me and thought at first that maybe I was imagining it.

We started talking about the stable first and all the ghostly phenomena that has occurred there over the years, but I could sense Rebecca's eagerness for us to get to her story. I tried to put the feelings I was having aside so that I could concentrate on the first part of the interview, but her presence next to me was so strong that I felt I had to reveal this to the group.

"I'm not surprised," Lynne said matter-of-factly. Things like this were nothing new to her, because Becca, as she was called by family and friends, found out how to communicate with her loved ones after her death.

"Becca Weissbard is a very strong spiritual presence," Joe said. "And she wants her story told."

Rebecca Weissbard grew up in Stony Brook and moved to Manorville with her family in 2005. She was the only daughter of Lynne, a horse trainer, and Eric, a firefighter and EMT. Lynne introduced horses to Becca early on, teaching her to ride at age three. Most children of that age would have to be led around by an adult, but not Becca. She took to the saddle almost immediately. By age four, Becca had begun her horse show career at Smoke Run Farm in Stony Brook, which was owned by George and Ruth Lukemire until it was sold in 2007. Lynne had worked at the stable as an equestrian camp counselor and began training her daughter for competition. Horses brought mother and daughter together in an inseparable bond, one that would last a lifetime and beyond.

Becca took riding seriously and had amazing confidence in her abilities as a rider. By the age of six, Becca was attending United States Equestrian Federation (USEF) shows and started winning ribbons.

"Becca was fearless," said Lynne. "Horses became her life, and she was happiest when she was riding."

When Lynne and Eric saw how passionate Becca was for the sport, they purchased their own stable and called it Sundance.

"Everything we did was to make Becca's riding career a reality," said Eric. "We were blessed with a child who had ability from the minute she sat on a horse. She had natural balance at age two. My entire life I worked two, sometimes three jobs to make it possible, and we bought a farm to make it happen. I sold my house and everything to get this place, which was a rundown cow farm, and make it a reality."

Lynne had trained Becca on ponies, and then other professional trainers were called in to help her advance to the junior hunter division. In 2007, Rebecca was Reserve Champion at the Hampton Classic Horse Show, and by 2008, she had started training with former equestrian Olympian Neil Shapiro in New Jersey. In 2011, she showed the Ocala, Florida Circuit with Neil Shapiro and became a serious competitor. She eventually returned home to finish high school and graduated from Eastport South Manor High School in Manorville in 2011. As she continued to pursue her riding career, she took up various student-type jobs, along with braiding horses for shows. The money she earned helped pay for horse show entrance fees.

Her work ethic and love for horses led her to a working student position with trainer Emil Spadone at the prestigious Redfield Farm, located in New Jersey. While there, she became a circuit champion in Amateur Hunters and became what is called a "catch rider" (riders who are asked to ride and show unfamiliar horses, oftentimes with very little notice).

"She loved a challenge, and she loved a difficult horse," said Lynne.

She returned to Neil Shapiro and his wife, Elisa, in the spring of 2013 so that she could train for the Maccabiah Games in Israel, which is the third largest sporting event in the world. Usually held the year following the Summer Olympics, the games are sanctioned by the International Olympic Committee and the World Federation of Sports. This year would be the first time the games would host equestrian events, and Becca wanted to be a part of it. Being the youngest rider to compete on the U.S. show team at age nineteen, Becca flew to Israel with Shapiro, coach of the American team, for the competition. Unfortunately, the horse she drew the day before the event came up lame, and she was forced to ride another horse with less than two hours of practice. Despite the misfortune, Becca landed herself an individual gold medal and helped the U.S. team win the team silver. It was at the Maccabiah Games that Becca was named America's Golden Girl.

Getting international recognition, Becca was offered a working student position at a noted international horse facility in Holland run by renowned trainer Loewie Joppen. She came back to the United States in 2014, with even more experience and a competition horse named Davarro. She made

Some of Rebecca's numerous awards.

Rebecca at the Maccabiah Games. *Photo courtesy of the Weissbard Family.*

one more trip back to Holland to ride in the fall of 2015, before arriving back home to compete and assist at her family's farm. Becca then trained with prominent rider and trainer Peter Leone, and she became a champion at many events.

The day she died, August 31, 2016, Rebecca had been with her mother at the prestigious HITS horse show in Saugerties, New York. She started off riding a junior rider's horse named Remember Me in a jumper division and ended up winning the class with a clean round and the fastest time. She did not know that she had won because an hour later she hopped on the horse of a friend to compete in another class. It was during this round that she had her fatal accident.

"The horse Becca was riding for someone else took off at the second jump and got caught up in the jump and flipped," Lynne began. "She fell free of the horse, but the horse flipped over and bounced and landed on her chest. She bled out right there."

Lynne paused and then continued. "I went into intense mode. I was all business. I was in the fire department, and I went to that place where you just try to do something, and nothing could be done."

"A parent's worst nightmare," I said.

"No, my worst nightmare was calling Eric and having to tell him. She was only twenty-two. Eric was on Long Island, and we were two hundred miles away. She was also the only grandchild on both sides of the family. How do you tell anybody that they lost their only grandchild?" Lynne paused. "I realized this [her death] was bigger than me. News of her death just exploded in the horse world and on social media. There were hundreds of her friends at this horse show too. There were so many signs though," Lynne remembered.

I was sitting at the morgue upstate, in the basement of the morgue, and I asked Rebecca to let me know that she was here. I felt this tingling on my arms. The hair just started sticking up on my arms. I knew she was there. I knew she was OK. She was always sending signs. There's been a lot of weird synchronicities and signs from Becca. About a year before Becca died, I had started to see numbers—333, 444, 555—a lot of numbers. On

Lynne Weissbard riding with large orb above her head. *Photo by Jeanie Leonard.*

the year anniversary of Becca's death, I saw a license plate in front of me on the way up to the horse show that Becca was killed at. ICU 126. The number she was wearing in the class she won and where she died was 621. So I see that number. And I saw it on the anniversary of her death, and I was like, "I see you too." I was seeing the number 621 even before I knew what it meant.

Lynne took a moment to gather her thoughts. "The two of us were so close. She was physically connected to me all the time, and this was huge for me because I was adopted, so I could never see my features in other people's faces," said Lynne. "I did with my daughter, and it was intense. I was there when she took her first breath, and I was there when she took her last. I was thirty feet away from her when she fell off. I feel like her soul was out of her body before she hit the ground because of the way she fell. Oddly enough, Rebecca always knew she was going to die young. She would say it. It's like she knew. Her favorite song was 'If I Die Young,' by the Band Perry. It was her ringtone."

"I've been a fireman for thirty-seven years," said Eric. "I've been an EMT for thirty-seven years. I've seen every sort of crazy thing you can imagine. I've seen every way a person can die. I've seen way too much stuff in my life. I was at the Trade Center. If there is a way for somebody to go to the hereafter, I've seen it. Up until Becca passed, nothing has ever bothered me. 9/11 affected me a lot and Becca's death. It made me different from what I was."

Eric then went on to explain an incident that happened one night after Becca's death.

"I was watching TV and dozed off. I woke up when I felt my foot being played with. I told Lynne to stop, but when I opened my eyes Lynne was not there. She was upstairs sleeping. So I open my eyes and I see a silhouette of a person with blond hair."

"I've had things happen when I'm sleeping," added Lynne. "One time I was sleeping, and something smacked me right square in the face. Like, boom! And I would wake up and there would be a horse loose outside that I would have to put away."

"That happens a lot," said Eric. "If something bad is going on outside, something will wake Lynne up. Another time one of the horses was sick. It was in real trouble. It's like a visitation from Becca."

Jeanie and Gerard knew Becca from when she was really young, and they watched her grow up. They were devastated by her death. Gerard believes he has gotten signs from Becca after her passing as well.

"I never get rid of contacts on my phone," said Gerard, "Especially a contact like Becca. I just couldn't get rid of it. My phone has been called by Becca a few times, and I answer it, but naturally, there's no one there, but I've been called by that number."

The group then went on to explain that Becca's ex-boyfriend had also been called by her number on occasion.

Becca was a mentor to other riders. She was fun, energetic, happy and full of life, and she was at the prime of her riding career when her accident took place. Her death had a profound effect on the Long Island riding community and beyond. Her funeral procession was so long that the Long Island Expressway was actually closed from Smithtown to Melville because the procession was two miles long.

A week or so after the funeral, the Weissbards organized a candlelight vigil at Sundance, where hundreds of people turned up to express their sympathy and to remember Becca.

Eric recalled:

> *People wanted to help. They wanted to give money. I didn't feel comfortable with doing something like a Go-Fund Me page. It was up to us to pay for her funeral. But people wanted to help, and I didn't want to use that money for us. So Lynne said we should do something to help others. We should help riders who have the ability to ride but can't necessarily afford it. People that ride here are working people and riding is a money sport. These kids want to ride because they love horses, but parents can't always afford it. So we created the Ride for Becca Foundation that helps children get the proper britches and boots so they fit in with the other riders, and it helps pay for lessons too. We have an old-fashioned country and western night every year with a DJ, fried chicken dinner and a barn dance. That's our big fundraiser, that and our Facebook fundraisers.*

Ride for Becca is an established 501(c)3 non-profit organization, and donations are tax deductible. The mission statement of the foundation is "Healing Horses, Hearts and Minds with the vision of finding the connection between kids with limited opportunities and unnoticed horses to foster mutual healing." Jeanie and Gerard have served on the foundation's board since it began.

Because Becca was such an inspiration to young riders, the Long Island Professional Horseman's Association Junior Committee created the Becca

Weissbard Award in her remembrance and offered an essay writing contest on "What does horsemanship mean to you?"

In 2017, almost a year after Becca's death, Lynne and Eric were invited back to the Maccabiah Games in Tel Aviv to help present a gold medal to a new rider in their daughter's honor. It was an amazing but bittersweet experience for the Weissbards.

With all of these things taking place after her death that have helped keep Becca's memory alive, how could she not find ways to communicate?

Joe had met Gerard Leonard at the Deepwells Haunted Mansion Tour in St. James in October 2017, and Gerard told him about the ghosts at Sundance Stable. Joe was invited to come to the barn a few weeks later and did a walk-around tour. He ended up doing an impromptu reading for the family, and Becca came through immediately. In the reading, Becca told Joe that her birthday was coming up, and to tell her parents not to forget her birthday. Joe confirmed with Eric that Becca's birthday was two weeks away. Becca also told Joe about an ugly blue riding helmet that her mother hated, and she told Joe about a horse she was with. Lynne told Joe that two horses had died, Mo and Daisy. Lynne and Eric asked Joe to ask Becca which horse was with her, to which Becca replied "Daisy." During the reading a thumping sound was heard in the house by everyone in the group. Becca then told Joe that she loved two books, *Rebecca of Sunnybrook Farms* and *National Velvet* and mentioned an old Shirley Temple movie on VHS. Eric confirmed that Becca had worn out the tape watching it. She told Joe about how she died in the riding accident and said she was already out of her body before the horse fell on her, something that Lynne had believed all along.

A few weeks after the family reading, a message circle was organized with Lynne's close friends, Becca's friends and equestrian clientele, along with two people from Joe's paranormal group. One of his group members captured an orb in the shape of an angel hovering over a house in the distance on North Street. It was snowing that night, and outside the window there were images of ghostly white horses gliding past the windows. This phenomenon, or morphing imagery, was seen by several members in the group. In addition, everyone heard heavy footsteps walking back and forth upstairs in the Weissbard house, where Becca's room had been located.

"Becca is a very loud spirit voice through the veil," said Joe. "I have experienced her presence off-site as well, recording responses from her at my residence with my ghost box."

Here is an excerpt from Joe's ghost box recording during the message circle in Manorville:

Joe: Becca, if you hear us say "hi."
Spirit: Here.
Joe: Here. Did you hear her say here?
Group: Yes.
Joe: What was your favorite horse's name, Becca?
Spirit: Love. Shooter.
Group: I heard Shooter!
Joe: Was that a horse's name?
Group: She hated Shooter.
[Group laughs.]
Joe: She hated Shooter.
[Joe laughs.]
Joe: Jeanie, you want to ask her something?
Jeanie: Becca, how is Shooter doing with me? How we doing riding?
Spirit: Perfect.
Gerard: I thought I heard perfect.
Joe: Perfect? Okay, good.
Jeanie: Which is not true, at all!
Spirit: You're kind.

Suddenly, the ghost box stops scanning at Becca's favorite Christmas song.

Song: Like a picture print by Currier and Ives—
Joe: Okay.
Song: These wonderful things are the things—
Eric: What movie is that from?
Lynne: Becca and I used to sing that song in the car.
Joe: Really? That song?
Lynne: All the time.
Group: Yeah.
Spirit: Not bad.
Joe: Not bad.
Joe: Talk to your father.
Spirit: Hi, Dad.
Joe: Hi, Dad. Did you hear that? Hi, Dad.

Joe, the Weissbards, the Leonards and Becca's friends are not the only ones who have had communication with Becca after her death. Along with the feeling of having Becca sitting in between Joe and me during our interview

Remember Becca.

at the stable, I had a few unexpected "visits" from her at my house. The first time was several hours after I arrived home from Manorville. The interview with Lynne and Eric had been intense, and I could feel their pain as they spoke. Being a mother and a former equestrian myself, Rebecca's story really hit home. I was heartbroken by what the Weissbards had lived through, and I was saddened by a life so young that was lost. In actuality though, I came to realize that her life was not lost.

I had taken all the papers, newspaper articles and stories about Becca's life up to my office and started reading them and looked at all the photographs of her. As I did, I couldn't help but well up with tears. Within a second, Rebecca was by my side. I heard her say, "Don't cry. I'm fine." I was taken aback thinking perhaps it was my mind playing tricks on me. I certainly don't have the abilities Joe has as a medium, but I knew beyond a shadow of a doubt that she was there and that she was happy. Rebecca came to me again when I started writing this story. I was considering a more sentimental opening paragraph, but I heard Becca say, "Get to the point, and start right in." So I did. I confirmed with Lynne that this was Becca's personality, to jump right in. As I began to write, I felt her presence on my left-hand side. After I finished the second paragraph, I heard her say, "Cool. This is cool."

Rebecca Weissbard lives on. She stays close to her family as she always did, and through her story, one can learn that life does exist beyond this one, and our loved ones never leave us. While on the earth, Rebecca lived her passion and her dream, and everyone who knew her loved her. What more could anyone ask for in a lifetime?

Life, if well lived, is long enough.
—*Lucius Annaeus Seneca*

BIBLIOGRAPHY

Beverly C. Tyler. "Three Village History, a House with a Long History." *Three Village Herald* (Setauket, NY), October 7, 1981.

Bleyer, Bill. *Long Island and the Sea: A Maritime History*. Charleston, SC: The History Press, 2019.

Brosky, Kerriann Flanagan. "Christmas at the Historic Milleridge Inn." *Edible Long Island*, November 18, 2015.

———. "Historic Milleridge Inn Saved!" *Edible Long Island*, December 4, 2015.

Cascone, Mary, with the Village of Babylon Historical and Preservation Society. *Babylon Village, Postcard History Series*. Charleston, SC: Arcadia Publishing, 2017.

Cow Neck Peninsula Historical Society. *Journals from 2015–2020*. Port Washington, NY, 2015–2020.

Forde, Barbara. "Frederick Bourne and the Long Island Maritime Museum." *Dolphin* 38, no. 1 (Winter 2007).

Fordyce, James. "Frederick Bourne and Indian Neck Hall." *Long Island Forum*, March 1987.

Hammond, John E. *Oyster Bay Remembered*. Huntington, NY: Maple Hill Press, 2002.

———. *Oyster Bay*. Charleston, SC: Arcadia Publishing, 2009.

Harrison, Joan, and Amy Dzija Driscoll. *Locust Valley*. Charleston, SC: Arcadia Publishing, 2012.

Henke, Hans. An assortment of research material on Lakeview Cemetery. Patchogue, NY.

————. *Patchogue: Queen City of Long Island's South Shore, the Early Years.* Blue Point, NY: AGC Printing & Design, 2003.

Huntington Historical Society. *Huntington Babylon Town History.* Huntington, NY: Huntington Historical Society, 1937.

Lapham, Edward A. *Stony Brook Secrets.* New York: Gotham Bookmart, 1942.

Lauer, Jean C. *Longwood, a History.* Brookhaven, NY: Town of Brookhaven Historical Advisory Committee, 1980.

————. *Longwood: An Historic Structure Report.* Setauket, NY: Society for the Preservation of Long Island Antiquities, 1984.

The Library—A Brief Review. Locust Valley, NY: Locust Valley Library, n.d.

Locust Valley Library Celebrating 100 Years 1909–2009. Locust Valley, NY: Locust Valley Library, 2009.

Locust Valley Library, Millennium Renewal Celebration, May 21, 2000. Locust Valley, NY: Locust Valley Library, 2000.

Magnani, Dorothy K. *Hamlet Study of Manorville.* Brookhaven, NY: Manorville Taxpayers Association, September 1993.

Magnani, Dorothy K., and Sandy Rafuse. *The History of Manorville.* Kearney, NE: Morris Publishing, 2007.

Meadow Croft Docent Guide. Sayville, NY: Bayport-Bluepoint Historical Association, 2019.

Muncy, Beulah. *Babylon Village History.* Babylon, NY: Babylon Village Historian, n.d.

"Obituary." *Sag Harbor Express,* September 16, 1875.

Oyster Bay Historical Society. *Walls Have Tongues, Oyster Bay Buildings and Their Stories.* Oyster Bay, NY: Oyster Bay Historical Society, 1999.

Patchogue Argus. "Mrs. Augusta J. Smith Weeks, a Philanthropic Woman Who Donated the Sailors Plot in Patchogue."

Society for the Preservation of Long Island Antiquities. *The Thompson House Setauket, NY.* Cold Spring Harbor, NY: SPLIA.

Stark, Thomas M. *Riverhead: The Halcyon Years 1861–1919.* Huntington, NY: Maple Hill Press, 2005.

The Story of the Brewster House, c. 1665 Also Known as the Joseph Brewster House. Setauket, NY: Ward Melville Heritage Organization.

Studenroth, Zachary N. *The Hawkins-Mount Homestead Historic Structure Report.* Stony Brook, NY: The Museums at Stony Brook, 1979.

Suffolk County. *Records of the Town of Brookhaven.* Suffolk County, NY: Burr Printing House, 1893.

Thompson, Benjamin F. *History of Long Island.* Vol. II. New York: R.H. Dodd, 1918.

"Unique Shaft Attests Her Pride in Smith Family." *Sunday World*, October 3, 1909.

United States Department of the Interior National Park Service. *National Register of Historic Places Inventory-Nomination Form Meadow Croft*. U.S. Government, 1987.

Ward Melville Heritage Organization. Various historical documents and notes on the Brewster House. Setauket, NY.

———. Various historical documents, notes and genealogy on the Thompson House. Setauket, NY.

Zaykowski, Dorothy Ingersoll. *The Old Burying Ground at Sag Harbor Long Island, New York*. Westminster, MD: Heritage Books, 2006.

Web Resources

Annibell, Wendy Polhemus. "Local History: Riverhead's Little Red Mill." Riverhead Local, www.riverheadlocal.com/2015/10/04/local-history-riveheads-little-red-mill.

"Cow Neck Historical Society Sands Willets House Tours." *Long Island Pulse.* www.lipulse.com/events/cow-neck-historical-society-sands-willets-house-tours.

Cow Neck Peninsula Historical Society. "Sands-Willets House." www.cowneck.org/sands-willets-house.

Greater Patchogue Historical Society. "*Louis V. Place* Shipwreck." www.greaterpatchoguehistoricalsociety.com.

History.com editors. "Meigs Expedition Claims Sole Patriot Victory on Long Island." A&E Television Networks, May 20, 2020, www.history.com/this-day-in-history/meigs-expedition-claims-sole-patriot-victory-on-long-island.

Ledda, Brianne. "Stony Brook Graves Lost to Memory, Buried in Time." *Statesman*, February 29, 2020. https://www.sbstatesman.com/2020/02/29/stony-brook-graves-lost-to-memory-buried-in-time/.

Long Island Genealogy. "Long Island Genealogy, *Louis V. Place*." www.longislandgenealogy.com/LouisVPlace.html.

Long Island Paranormal Investigators. "Lakeview Cemetery." www.liparanormalinvestigators.com/haunted-places-on-li/suffolk-county/lake-view-cemetery.

Long Island Stories. "Lakeview Cemetery." www.sites.google.com/site/longislandstories/whose-haunting-lakeview-cemetery.

Long Island Trail Lovers Coalition. "Riverhead: Cranberry Bog Preserve County Park." https://www.litlc.org/trails/riverhead/cranberry.htm.

Loughlin Vineyard. "Our History. Where It All Began." www.loughlinvineyardny.com/our-history.

Milleridge Inn. "The History of Milleridge and the Architecture of Milleridge." www.milleridgeinn.com.

Muller, James. "Save American History! Save the Historic 340 Year Old Milleridge Inn." Save the Milleridge Facebook Page.

O'Keefe, Michael. "Dix Hills Man Charged with Uncles Killing, Cops Say." *Newsday*. www.newsday.com/long-island/crime/arrest-fatal-stabbing-levittown.

Riverhead, New York website. "Riverhead History." www.townofriverheadny.gov.

Sag Harbor Old Burying Ground Committee. "About the Burying Ground." www.sagharboroldburyingground.wordpress.com.

Sag Harbor Partnership. "Sag Harbor in Wartime." www.sagharborpartnership.org/sag-harbor-in-wartime.html.

Tyler, Beverly C. "Mounts Discovered Slave History in Stony Brook Graveyard." TBR News Media, March 2, 2018. https://tbrnewsmedia.com/mounts-discovered-slave-history-stony-brook- graveyard.

Underhill. "Old Burying Ground, Sag Harbor." Carol's House. https://carolshouse.com/cemeteryrecords/oldburyingground.

Unknown Gender History (blog). "The Unknown History of Misandry: Helen Tiernan, Hatchet Murderess Whose Kids were in the Way." March 13, 2015. www.unknownmisandry.blogspot.com/2011/07/helen-tiernan-hatchet-murderess-whose.html.

Vespe, Elizabeth. "Sag Harbor's Old Whalers' Church, Once the Tallest Structure on Long Island." *27East*, May 14, 2019. www.27east.com/southampton-press/sag-harbors-old-whalers-church-once-the-tallest-structure-on-long-island-celebrates-175-years-1590018.

Virgintino, Mike. "The Battle of Sag Harbor in the War for Independence." Classic New York History. www.classicnewyorkhistory.com/the-battle-of-sag-harbor-in-the-war-for-Independence.

Ward Melville Heritage Organization. "Brewster House." www.wmho.org/attractions/the-brewster-house-c-1665.

The Witching Hour (blog). "Haunted Long Island: The Milleridge Inn." www.4girlsandaghost.wordpress.com/2011/10/17haunted-long-island-the-milleridge-inn.

Other

Written and acquired documents and docent guide on Babylon's history and the history of the Nathaniel Conklin House, courtesy of Mary Cascone and the Conklin House Committee. The authors and sources from these materials are unknown.

About the Author

Award-winning author and historian Kerriann Flanagan Brosky is the author of nine books and has been featured in numerous publications including the *New York Times*, *Newsday* and *Distinction* magazine. She has appeared on CBS *Sunday Morning*, *Ticket* with Laura Savini, News 12 Long Island and the Thinking Writer in East Hampton. Kerriann served on the Board of Trustees as first vice president for the Huntington Historical Society for six years, and she served as a trustee for the Greenlawn-Centerport Historical Association for three years. Kerriann is the recipient of the Top Advocate for Historic Preservation and Education award from the Oyster Bay Historical Society, the Huntington Heritage Education Award from the Town of Huntington and Woman of Distinction award from the New York State Assembly. Kerriann is also a food writer and was a contributing writer for *Edible Long Island* for five years, where she had her own column, "Kerriann Eats." Kerriann is president emeritus of the Long Island Authors Group and is a well-known speaker who draws standing-room-only crowds to her lectures. Please visit her website at *www. kerriannflanaganbrosky.com*.

ABOUT THE CONTRIBUTOR

 oe Giaquinto is a psychic-medium and paranormal investigator. He has experienced paranormal phenomena for over forty years. In 2005, Joe discovered his gift of mediumship. Today, he uses this ability to conduct group and private readings and for analyzing and corroborating paranormal evidence in the field. Joe graduated magna cum laude from Adelphi University. He currently manages a freelance computer consulting/web-design business. His professional memberships have included the American Society for Psychical Research, Association TransCommunication, Forever Family Foundation, Hampton Bays Historical Society, First Parish Church and the Ghost Hunters of Long Island. Joe has appeared on numerous cable TV and radio shows and in online and print newspapers. He has given professional presentations, lectures and workshops for private organizations, historical societies, public libraries, holistic learning centers and private businesses. Since 2005, Joe has collaborated with Kerriann Flanagan Brosky on several Long Island book projects about ghosts. Visit Joe at *www.joegmediumpi.com*.